Praise For Harry Was Right All Along

"A refreshing and thought-provoking insight into the rapidly evolving high street by a skilled practitioner"
Lord Mark Price, Founder, Engaging Works, former Managing Director, Waitrose, and Deputy Chairman, John Lewis Partnership

"Andrew pulls no punches in his assessment of what's going wrong in retail. The inclusion of articles he's written previously are a reminder of his foresight both in relation to what happened and why but also provide a perspective of what's to come in retail. I also really like the under-lying premis of the book that we could all do with reflecting on what made Harry Selfridge such a success when he opened Selfridges. We too often forget about the retail basics of having the right products, presented well with great service"
Martin Newman, Founder of The Customer First Group

"Andrew Busby is one of our most insightful retail commentators, and it is great to have these collected thoughts on the unprecedented changes taking place in retailing today, driven by our ever more demanding and promiscuous customers. Whether it is discussing the parallels between retailing and motor racing, attacking the 'amorphous aberration' of business rates, or exploring the importance of personalisation and artificial intelligence, Busby is consistently interesting and thought-provoking, and I take comfort in his conclusion that there is a bright future for those of us who can adapt to offer shopping as 'a social and experiential activity' capable of meeting the needs of Generation Z. Which is satisfyingly close to what Harry (Selfridge) offered to London 110 years ago, proving him - as the title states - right all along"
Richard Walker, Managing Director, Iceland Foods

"It's completely right that Andrew has dedicated this book to everyone who works in retail - past, present and future - as they are the heroes of the straight-talking insight he shares so eloquently"
Helen Dickinson OBE, Chief Executive, British Retail Consortium

"It is packed with the sort of insights that can only come from long experience and reflection on the retail industry. It is also rich in practical examples of retailers – many of them independent business owners - who are bucking the negative trend by following old-fashioned principles, which have never been more relevant"
Mark Pilkington, Former CEO, Kamal Osman Jamjoom

HARRY WAS RIGHT ALL ALONG

Who Was Harry And What Can He Teach Us About Retail Today?

A Collection Of Short Stories From The High Street

Andrew Busby

Dedicated to all those who work in the retail industry

CONTENTS

FOREWORD 1
INTRODUCTION 3
PART ONE: GREAT EXPECTATIONS 5
    Consumer Expectations Of Retailers Are Rising, But Will They Pay? 12
    M&S Sells Great Food, But Simply Dull Clothes 13
    What Women Want And Why You Should Pay Attention To Them 15
    You May Have Won My Mind, Amazon, But Not My Heart 17
    Calling Julian Dunkerton At Superdry, You're No Longer In Fashion 19
    Forget Customer Experience, Boris Johnson Will See To That 21
PART TWO: I AM THEREFORE I SHOP 23
    The Human Touch Is Central To Brand Experience 27
    Is Your Retail Model Set Up For Baby Boomers, Not Millennials? 28
    Five Reasons Why The Department Store Model Is Far From Dead 30
    Black Friday Blues: Is The Annual Orgy Of Excess Losing Its Appeal? 32
    Massive, Fun and Cheap. Why The New Primark Store In Birmingham Is Sure To Succeed 34
    Shoppers Secretly Being Filmed The Shocking Truth Behind Retailers Tricking Us Into Buying More 36
    The Shop Now, Pay Later Model Is Gaining Popularity: Here's Why 38
PART THREE: CUSTOMER FIRST, NO REALLY 40
    Toastie Wars! 43
    A Modern Day Arkwright, A Retail Journey Back To The Future 45
    Why Retailers Need To Remain Relevant 47
    The Mary Poppins Of Retail How One Apprentice Star Created A Retail Phenomenon 49
    The Sweet Smell Of Success 51
    How Did I Do? 53
    Love Them Or Loathe The, Serial Returners Could Just Be Your Best Customers 55
    What Barbados Can Teach Sainsbury's And UK Supermarkets 57
PART FOUR: IT'S A BUSINESS ISSUE 59
    Why Brands Fail 62

One Bad Apple?...64

Bungled Bunnings - A Case For Review...66

Five Things We Learnt At Retail Week Live...67

Weather: Are You Getting It?..70

The Famous Five - How To Survive Today's Retail Storm 72

Why Your Most Important Asset Is Out There Now Representing Your Brand 75

From The Dalai Lama To Hostage Negotiation: A Meeting With Jacqueline de Rojas
....77

As Kingfisher Parts Company With Its CEO The Question Is, What Does Plan B Look Like?..79

The Reverse Ferret And The Department Store: How Today Became Debs Day..........80

Bonmarché: Is Private Equity The Real Reason For The Death Of The High Street? .82

Why The CMA Were Wrong And Where Now For Sainsbury's And Asda?..................84

Landlords Braced To Be Hit By The Retail Transformation..........................86

Why The Demise Of Arcadia Is Bad News For All Of Us..............................88

PART FIVE: THE PATIENT NEEDS MORE THAN LIFE SUPPORT 90

Black Friday Blues 92

NRF 2018 - A Look Ahead 94

NRF Day One: Retail Rallying Cry..96

NRF Day 2: Meet The Future Of Retail...98

NRF Day 3: Saving The Best Till Last 100

Are We Killing The High Street? 102

Business Rates: The Curse Of The High Street..103

Why The Budget Does Virtually Nothing For UK Retailers 105

Retail 2019: Time To Get Back To Basics..107

A Brexit Boxset And Why It Is Such An Uncertain Time For Retail 108

Why Brexit Is Proving Disastrous For Retail 111

MPs Report On The High Street Falls Short..113

Arcadia And An Austin Allegro Have More In Common Than You Might Think ...115

PART SIX: OLD RETAIL, NEW TRICKS...117

Start-ups Continue To Innovate Delivery Options For Retailers.................120

Crack It With Cognitive...122

Enhanced Automation And Why Our Skies Won't Be Filled With Drones 124

How Social Media Influence Will Increasingly Affect Retail Success	126
Why Jimmy Choo Is A Good Fit For Michael Kors	128
Why Christmas Ads Must Pass The Goosebump Test	129
Embrace Change – And Do It Now	131
Why The Time Is Now For The Forgotten Technology Of Retail	133
The Retail Perfect Storm And Why Old Retail Is Broken Forever	135
The Ghost Of Retail Yet To Come	137
M&S Turns To Investors To Buy Into Online Grocery Market	139
New PwC Survey Reveals Consumer Data Is The Most Highly Valued	141
Iceland Foods – More Than You Think	142
PART SEVEN: PHOENIX	**144**
eBay's Emotion Store Gives A Glimpse Into The Future	145
A Fabulously British Affair At Jack Wills	146
The Times They Are A-Changin'	147
Thirty Million Bubbles	149
Everyone's Welcome	151
New Thinking Needed For Healthy High Streets	152
Jack's: Back To The Future?	154
Artificial Intelligence: Saint Or Sinner?	155
Best Of Times, Worst Of Times: What Does 2019 Have In Store For Retail?	157
High Velocity Retail: Why The World Retail Congress Was A Breath Of Fresh Air	159
Why A Few Less Boots On The High Street Can Only Be Healthy	161
From Opening His Own Bookstore To Running Barnes & Noble, The Incredible Journey Of James Daunt	162
AFTERWORD	**164**

FOREWORD

It was Brands Hatch, the famous motor racing circuit in Kent, a few years ago and I had qualified my BMW M3 on the front row of the grid. To say I was pleased with the way the day had gone so far would be an understatement. Problem was, behind me were 30 other hooligans all chomping at the bit to go as soon as the red lights went out. And out they went but whilst everyone else floored it and accelerated off the grid, I went nowhere. A clutch problem meant I couldn't get it in gear and whilst frantically trying to rectify this I was swamped by everyone. I've never been so scared in all my life, the chances of being hit – and hit very hard – were extremely high. Those at the back of the grid would be doing close on 100mph by the time they reached me and the result of contact would be one very second hand car not to mention the driver (I've never liked hospital food).

Thankfully, miraculously, they all somehow managed to avoid me but the experience is not one I'd ever wish to repeat! So, this got me thinking about my twin passions – retail and motorsport – and the similarities between the two. Perhaps not obvious at first glance but nevertheless take a closer look and they become all too apparent.

Never more has this been the case than in motorsport where competition and competitiveness are often at the outer limits of the scale. Quite sane, seemingly normal people can grow horns when they get behind the wheel of a racing car. And will equally spend completely crazy amounts of money just to go that little bit quicker. It's in the blood you see.

But what of retail? Observing the High Street of today, the competition between retailers is fierce and cut throat – not an inch given to their rivals and all fiercely protective of their territory. It's survival of the fittest – just like on the track where a moment's hesitation can cost you a place or worse. Teamwork – synonymous with motorsport and perhaps motorsport is the ultimate team sport. A dropped catch in cricket or a missed penalty in football carry a certain level of consequence however if a mechanic fails to tighten the wheel nuts properly the results can be disastrous.

Trust in one's fellow team members is absolute and paramount. Never more so than in retail where, in today's world every aspect of the organisation is linked in a way never before realised. From supply chain to merchandising to eCommerce to marketing each part must operate together in perfect harmony as opposed to working in silo's, each focused on their own individual goals and targets. This is a real challenge for many retailers today – to maintain good retail discipline and trusted metrics - key performance indicators (KPIs) whilst embracing the modern era of retailing where the whole organisation must work together with a collective focus on the customer in order to deliver an amazing experience time and time again.

I fear it will be a step too far for some. Not quite the scenario in retail but the similarity in terms of the pace of development and change holds true. Nothing stands still and in retail, just as in motor racing; standstill and you go backwards. Never before has the pace of change, driven by technology, been so relentless. It is mind blowing. And with cognitive computing and artificial intelligence this is only set to accelerate. Those who do not adopt the latest technology in order to drive deep, insightful and relevant personalisation, will find themselves without a business before very long. Over the years many Formula One teams have withered and died, caught out by the pace of development and left behind, the same is true for retail brands.

I have a profound respect and admiration for anyone who, out of choice, would wish to be the CEO of a retail brand these days. Personally, I think they must in some way be slightly unhinged, caught as they are between the twin pressures of keeping the business on track whilst at the same time constantly having to develop new parts for the business and bring them onstream faster than the competition. But just like in motorsport – where it is said, if you want to be a millionaire just start out with £2 million - it is the passion for retail which drives these CEOs on.

And that is why, just like my motor racing heroes, I admire them so much for they operate in a rarefied place where just one slip, one lapse in concentration can have disastrous consequences.

INTRODUCTION

Sometimes I shop on the internet, you just might do too. It is a truth that our collective shopping habits are changing at a rapid rate; that much we know. Change has never been so relentless but whilst this will inevitably lead to casualties, this is all part of the process of the changing of the guard. Because just as in nature, the strongest will survive and the weak are culled in order for the herd to survive and thrive. We are in the midst of witnessing the same process of evolution within retail. Crucially, it cannot do it all on its own; retail needs help and needs help now.

The crippling and outdated business rates tax burden which traditional (bricks and mortar) retailers are faced with is an amorphous aberration, devised as it was in 1988. That's six years before Amazon was introduced to the world and nearly twenty before the first iPhone was launched. Hard to believe but back then we had yet to enjoy the convenience of shopping online but whilst online grew and grew, the system of taxing retail businesses has remained steadfastly stuck in the eighties.

But rather than dwell on the challenges facing retail (for they have been expertly documented elsewhere) this book is meant, through a collection of short stories, to be a celebration of retail, a means by which we can shine a light on the greatest industry of all without being naïve to the pressures it is experiencing like never before.

If Harry was right all along, just who was Harry? I took inspiration from the great Harry Gordon Selfridge, who was a retail genius. In today's language, it is all about 'experiential' retail (oh, how I loathe that word!) and putting the customer first - as if there was a time when we didn't do that? Over a hundred years ago Harry Selfridge was espousing these things, treating his customers as guests and his famous store on Oxford Street as a place for people to gather and socialise and to be inspired. Sounds familiar? He was truly ahead of his time. It's just that it has taken the majority of retailers time to catch on. But catch on they are now doing, driven by a new, expectant breed of consumer, the like of which we've never seen before.

So, this, my first book, is a collection of tales, anecdotes and observations on retail, the consumer and the high street. We seem to be continuously bombarded with the retail apocalypse narrative, one which I personally don't subscribe to. And for that reason, part seven is titled 'Phoenix' because for me, that is what we are currently witnessing in retail. Yes, it is changing, yes, the future won't be the same and yes, we are currently witnessing a period of unparalleled transformation. Because that is what it is: transformation. We, the consumer, are evolving our shopping habits at a pace never before envisaged. That smartphone in our pockets has given us the power and the global financial crisis of 2008, the incentive to become the savvy consumer which we now see on every high street and on every website.

Challenging, tough, exciting, stimulating, frustrating, scary – retail today is all of these things and more. Which is why those working in this fantastic industry are the lucky ones. Careers are being defined, brands are being born and growing at a rate never before seen. And whilst administrations, store closures, company voluntary arrangements (CVA's), business rates and the impact of Brexit on consumer confidence grab all the headlines, retail still remains the most rewarding and relevant industry. We have emotional attachments with our favourite retail brands which we simply don't with other sectors. Don't you just love it when your utility supplier sends you a little more gas or electricity? No, of course you don't!

But retail is different in that it is the most visible and the one sector with which we develop these emotional bonds. Over ten years after falling into administration, people still talk fondly of Woolworths. Retailers have a place in our lives like no other. And whilst the entire industry is being challenged from all sides to grow and evolve – possibly in ways we have yet to imagine – the very essence of it will remain the same. Serving the customer, putting the customer first, earning our trust and respect. For that reason, this book is dedicated to everyone who works in retail - past, present and future. I admire and respect you all. I hope you enjoy this, my personal collection of tales from the high street.

PART ONE: GREAT EXPECTATIONS

People often ask; what is the biggest disruptor in retail? But this of course, is the wrong question because what they should be asking is not what but *who* is the biggest disruptor in retail? And the answer to that question is you, me – all of us. Because as consumers, our expectations are growing exponentially at a rate which is far outstripping retailers' ability to keep pace.

Our demands and expectations are almost out of control, the last great experience simply raising the bar ever higher and this is driving a tsunami of change throughout retail which shows no sign of abating. The implications for every retail business are profound and must be faced up to in order to survive. At the time of writing, many retail businesses are under severe pressure to survive, Debenhams being the latest to agree a company voluntary agreement (CVA) in order to close stores and reduce the rent burden on the remainder. This is now practically becoming accepted practice and nothing out of the ordinary. The same appears to be true of Arcadia whose flagship Topshop brand has been struggling to keep the rest of the ship afloat for some time now.

And why mention these two especially when there are many others which could have been included? Because they both have two things in common: they are both suffering from a lack of investment in ecommerce years ago and, partly as a consequence, both have lost their relevance. And it is relevance that trumps discounting every time. We have been educated to expect certain characteristics when shopping online. Amazons one-click online experience being a case in point. That has set the bar for ease and convenience of the online experience and so, quite justifiably, we expect the same from any of our online shopping experiences. The same goes for delivery which is rapidly moving towards same day being the norm. And this is perhaps the new battleground for retailers. I predict that final mile delivery capabilities will come to define a retail brand. In this era of great expectations, we will soon be expecting anytime, anywhere delivery not just same day but within the hour in many cases.

Matchesfashion.com are a case in point. If you live in central London and order online, they proudly boast that you will be wearing the garment within ninety minutes. How long before that becomes 'within the hour'? Where does it all end? Artificial Intelligence (AI) is learning all the time and therefore learning all the time about us, our habits, our preferences. Scary, intrusive – maybe, but ultimately this will drive an era of hyper personalisation where retailers and brands will be able to predict what we want or need before we even realise it ourselves. Ironically, the only barrier to this will be the same disruptor which is driving it: us. GDPR has shone a spotlight on personal data and the need to keep private what needs to be kept private. It will be fascinating to watch over the coming years how this develops as our initial fears of being 'slaves to the algorithm' dissipate in the face of ever more convenience.

Frictionless and seamless are terms both used (too often in my opinion) to describe the ideal shopping experience. And, of course for commodity items both would apply if they are interpreted to mean ease, speed and convenience. This goes for both the online and the physical shopping journeys. And in the case of the latter, I don't subscribe to the notion that self-service checkouts in supermarkets improve customer experience. For those of a certain age (such as myself) I can still remember my very first job as a petrol pump forecourt attendant. Yes, my job was to fill customers cars with fuel. They would have recoiled in horror if I'd said, 'nah mate, fill it up yourself'! But the oil companies gradually educated us to expect to have to get out of our cars often in the freezing cold, get our hands on a grubby fuel hose and then have to queue behind people seemingly doing their weekly shop. Shell brought back attended service at their stations at certain times and I was struck by my reaction when a Shell forecourt attendant approached me recently offering to fill the car up for me. I was quite taken aback and eyed him with suspicion. No, I'll do it myself thank you very much. Oh, how times change!

Soon we won't see any attended checkouts in supermarkets, and there are those who believe that the Amazon Go model will become the norm for all supermarkets. Walk in, fill our basket and walk out. And it is to stores that we turn to explore perhaps the one area where our expectations are driving seismic changes. Harry was indeed right when he said "excite the mind and the hand will reach for the pocket". Stores, more than ever, need to inspire, excite and intrigue us, with a new surprise around every corner. Selfridges on Oxford Street is the epitome of this but others are also realising that whilst in the future there may be less, stores, the ones which remain must be magical places to spend time. The new Primark in Birmingham, which at the time of writing is their largest in the world, is a case in point. Stretching the boundaries of the brand in ways least expected such as a barber's, a beauty salon and restaurants. Whilst online continues to grow (some experts putting it as consuming anything up to 35% of all our spend before plateauing out) it is to the physical stores we turn to for that exciting, inspiring experience. After all, as boss of Boxpark, Roger Wade once put it; "online is like watching fireworks on TV".

The store is dead, long live the store

Never has the High Street been more competitive, never has it been so dynamic and demanding and most importantly, never have we as consumers been more demanding of retailers. Can retailers afford to continue to innovate, deliver great product and at rock bottom prices whilst at the same time deliver a truly memorable customer experience? And if the last is true, what one ingredient will facilitate this?

Austerity has had many varying impacts on both the economy and our spending habits, none more so than on the High Street where it has changed behaviour for good. Loyalty, if it ever existed, certainly doesn't today – except at point of purchase - and so as we become ever more promiscuous in our shopping behaviour so too must retailers strive ever increasingly to convince us to part with our hard-earned cash. It is this mixture of intense competitiveness, highly dynamic and ever-changing landscape combined with not only a lack of any loyalty but acute consumer expectation which is creating a maelstrom for retailers, the like of which has never been witnessed before. So how can a retailer hope to differentiate themselves and create a compelling offer for the consumer?

We now take cheap, inexpensive grocery, electrical and fashion items for granted. We expect that they will be available when and where we want them; delivered to our place of choice without trouble or fuss. In short, we expect ease and convenience – much of which is of course online and many column inches are devoted to online, omni-channel, multi-channel – call it what you will. However, the fascination now is not online but the role which the bricks and mortar store estate plays in all of this. How a retailer differentiates through their physical presence will in the next few years, come to define the success of their online offering.

Imagine a world which was 100% online? No shops except for showrooms in which to view the product before buying. It simply couldn't exist; shopping is intrinsically a social and experiential activity and this will never change. In addition, it is sensory and retailers know this – especially fashion retailers where, if you've ever noticed, all our senses are engaged in the buying process. But all this is to ignore the one key factor which will redefine the retail industry in the coming years – its staff.

Traditionally, retail has not been viewed as a great career option in the same way as, for instance, banking once was. With the perfect storm of fierce competition, the need for great in-store customer experience, together with the necessity to drive for better efficiency and productivity, no longer will store staff be seen as a necessary cost. They will become the front line leading the brand, able to create a memorable and great experience unlike no other. Retail will undergo a major transformation in the way that it promotes itself to young people, offering career paths like never before, showing that whether it be in retail operations, supply chain, buying, merchandising, there awaits a great career path in retail far beyond the popular zero hours filler jobs whilst waiting for something better to come along. For all those having received their A level results and considering their University options, retail should be high on the list.

Why brand loyalty is a myth

Consumer expectations take many forms. We've looked at online, stores and delivery but what of loyalty? Think of your shopping habits compared with 10 years ago. Are they any different today? Chances are they are. And in what way?

The most striking difference will most likely be in your loyalty (or otherwise) to particular retailers or brands. Because back then, the global financial crisis was just about to hit us and smartphones were in their infancy. What we didn't realise is that these two things would revolutionise not just our shopping behaviour but our attitude to brands. Whereas before we would behave in a manner more reflecting our parents - those born in the baby boomer years (and before) - who gathered 'stuff' in a manner which bemuses current day millennials.

That global financial crisis not only dented our already fragile confidence in bankers, it fundamentally shifted our belief systems. No more were we slaves to whatever was pushed in our direction. And then the consumer finally came of age - and with that smartphone in our pockets, we had the means by which to exercise our new found consumer confidence. We flexed our muscles and exerted our influence on retail brands; long since bloated on the idea that they could simply stack their shelves and we would come calling. The financial crisis gave us the incentive, that smartphone in our pockets provided us with the tool and social media the platform by which we could finally exert pressure on retailers.

I often look at my own personal shopping behaviour to inform me and whilst I naturally see the world through my own lens (we all see the world from our own perspective) after years of observing, with quiet admiration, I recently made my first purchase from a certain fashion retailer who would like us to believe that it has a Japanese heritage. I was in need of a new winter jacket and was very satisfied to find the one I wanted. But after only two weeks of use, the zip completely gave out. £85 worth of jacket pretty much binned. Both emotionally and psychologically I was ready to commit my (albeit limited) loyalty to this brand. And yet now I feel let down, almost betrayed that this commitment has in some way been for nothing.

This is likely to be my last experience with this particular brand; the unwritten consumer - retailer trust agreement has been broken. Tolerance and patience are virtues not commonly associated with consumers these days. Our expectations demand that our relationships with brands has fundamentally shifted. Rationally, I can understand that these things happen. But emotionally, it is a different story. The relationship between consumer and retailer today is more tenuous and fragile than ever. Loyalty is a thing of the past. Today we are far less tolerant, less forgiving and certainly less patient with retailers and brands than ever before. And one thing is clear; give customers a reason to follow your brand and they'll do so willingly. Give them a reason to dislike it and they'll drop you like a ton of bricks.

Why you need a happy workforce

But our expectations aren't just limited to price, product, online, delivery capability or the appearance of the store. There is one ingredient which we haven't touched on yet but is one that can make or break a brand: people. Or to be more precise, a retailer's store staff. As stores move into a new era of being, as Howard Saunders the Retail Futurist, aptly describes, becoming 'playgrounds', the days of simply stocking and selling 'stuff' are well and truly over. One thing's for sure, if your business involves human interaction, you need your greatest asset - your workforce - to be as happy as they possibly can be. Here's why. But first a tale familiar to many of us.

I approached the checkout with a degree of trepidation. OK so the self-service checkout was available but today the prospect of yet another battle of wills with a soulless automated machine was not one I relished. That could wait for another time. For a change, what I sought on this occasion was some human interaction - a smiling face, a cheery hello - a smooth and pleasant transition from store navigation to satisfied customer. The experience was anything but.

My greeting was met with an eye contactless grunt. Request for payment was something indecipherable. A relatively enjoyable shopping experience had quickly been undermined at the last but crucial stage. This left me wondering; is this person that unhappy to be at work? I can't think of another industry which thrives on as much human contact as retail and hospitality.

Think of your last stay in a hotel. What defined the experience? The surroundings? The room? The food? I'm sure all of the above contributed however I would argue that one aspect in particular can make a good hotel great and a great hotel average: the staff. I've been fortunate to stay at some wonderful hotels; one in particular however - the Chewton Glen in the New Forest - stands out.

Consistently ranked as one of the top hotels in the world, it may not be the most expensive, but it is most certainly, for me at least, one of, if not the best. Why? Put simply - it is 100% down to the staff. They absolutely and completely define the hotel. From the Manager to the Chambermaid it is easy, relaxed, pleasant, friendly - polished. It is the stuff of dreams, as if the very fabric of the hotel has been sprinkled with fairy dust and in doing so a wonderful, magical experience is created for their guests. So, if people can make or break your brand, isn't it something worth paying a little attention to? We'll revisit the wonderful Chewton Glen in part four.

Customers come second

"Staff first, customers second and shareholders third. In this order, everyone is kept happy. It's our people who drive our success, so we strive to maintain a healthy and happy culture"

Sir Richard Branson

This might sound a little counter intuitive however it's the way that Virgin, under Richard Branson, treats its customers. But who would argue with the logic? If there is a direct link between employee happiness and business success wouldn't it be great if there was a way to easily and quickly, not only measure but improve employee happiness? Engaging Works, the brainchild of former Waitrose MD Lord (Mark) Price, does just this.

Working on the principle that happier employees are more engaged employees hence are more productive, provide better customer experience and in so doing become more fulfilled people both at work and at home. "All the research shows that the companies with more engaged workforces are more profitable, more productive, and more successful" states Lord (Mark) Price. I predict that employee happiness will feature ever more strongly on the radars of retailers eager to retain and grow their customer base as they realise that their people are their most valuable asset. As consumer expectations and demands continue to increase, it's the human touch which will differentiate the great brands from the merely good.

Stores no longer simply sell stuff

I referred to Howard Saunders earlier when he talked about stores becoming 'playgrounds' and not simply selling 'stuff. It's worth exploring this a little further because it has significant implications for all physical retailers (which of course is the vast majority). Because if you think your stores are there to just sell stuff; stop reading now. If, on the other hand, you view your stores as being a little more than just a glorified warehouse, let me explain.

Because in an era when our expectations are like a freight train in danger of running out of control, ever more imaginative ways to present the store are needed. And perhaps the newest trend in retail is....not to sell anything. Well, directly that is; for it seems that in the rapid evolution of stores the idea now goes far beyond stock churn and ringing tills. Because in today's retail, the smart money eschews the idea of shifting any product up front.

For some time now, upmarket cycling brand, Rapha, have referred to their stores as 'clubhouses', places where the sweaty, lycra-clad faithful can commune and share stories with other, well, sweaty, lycra-clad enthusiasts. A place not to come and buy but to discuss the relative merits of Shimano versus Campagnolo over an espresso or two. Personally, the thought of middle-aged men squeezing their ever-burgeoning waistlines into an outfit more suited to a gymnast fills me with horror. But Rapha has tapped into this middle-aged market and rather than simply selling cycling gear, they offer their 'clubhouses' as places where fellow enthusiasts can gather together. And frankly, they do it really rather well. You see, Harry was right all along.

Just hanging out

Alternative in-store experiences are nothing new of course, it's just that they're getting better. Eight years ago, in their flagship Currys stores, Dixons were showing off their kitchen equipment by having trained chefs cooking up something delicious.

This is a very exciting time to be a consumer because the entire concept of the role of the store has been taken to a different level. Lululemon began yoga classes in its stores a number of years ago and this now extends to their 'Sweat with Us' events. Forget the website, forget the store even, because there's a whole brand world out there just waiting to be explored. Opened in early 2019, at the Nike 'House of Innovation' store on 5th Avenue in New York, they are able to produce a completely customised pair of trainers for you within the hour.

This development of the brand experience hasn't escaped the luxury end of the market either. Why? Because, according to Fashionista, the hot new trend in luxury fashion is not selling anything. From Hermes to Dolce and Gabbana, brands are creating both permanent and pop-up spaces just for us to go and hang out. Hermès, one of the most exclusive and luxurious brands, opened "Carré Club" (carré meaning "scarf") pop-ups in New York, Toronto, Singapore, Los Angeles and Milan. With free public admission, guests could get photos taken, sing karaoke (sorry, Carré-Ok), enjoy complimentary refreshments from a café and watch artists and designers at work. In London, the aforementioned Matchesfashion.com opened 5 Carlos Place, a Mayfair townhouse with a retail component that serves as a community space where all sorts of event programming takes place, as well as live streaming and podcasts for those who can't visit it in person.

Click bait's the new name in town for 2019; making your stores 'Instagram ready' is vital if you want your brand to stand out because this is where your influencers expect to come and just hang with your brand because, dude, well, just because. But it's when they start snapping and sharing, you just know what all their followers are going to do; that, my friend, is when you sell. Stores must be so much more than, well, just stores these days; as consumers we expect it.

Consumer Expectations Of Retailers Are Rising, But Will They Pay?

First published in Retail Week, 9 February 2015

Click and collect, home delivery, WiFi, personalisation, RFID, tablets, ever lower prices, condensed lead times…the list goes on but all these are what are now expected by consumers. Shoppers have got used to high quality, low priced food, they've got used to buying a pair of jeans for £10, used to being able to order by 10pm and have the item delivered to the location of our choice the next day. Service levels are ever increasing but consumers expect prices to stay low. The question is whether this model sustainable for the retailers?

The news that Bank was the first casualty of 2015 may have come as little surprise and the fact remains that each January, we see some retail names going to the wall in the aftermath of peak trading. This year pressure was even heavier, with the increasing popularity amongst consumers of the so-called Black Friday, an unwanted US phenomenon which artificially creates demand and places huge pressures on retailers.

Such was the impact in 2014 that Andy Street, boss of retail bellwether John Lewis, was moved to say "we've got to ask if it's right to concentrate trade so much in that one period" and "my personal hope is that this is the high-water mark for Black Friday. I don't think we can put the genie back in the bottle but do we need to stoke that fire anymore? I personally hope not".

If such excessive consumer expectations are beginning to worry the likes of John Lewis, what impact must all this be having on the smaller retailers?
Are consumers unwittingly creating a landscape where collective expectations are placing an unsustainable burden on retailers such that it will ultimately drive them out of business? Because at the moment it seems that the one differentiator a retail brand has left up its sleeve is customer experience, but are shoppers expecting too much? Grocers struggle to make much money out of home delivery, so why do they provide the service? Click & collect is currently the darling of many consumers. What could be better? Well, quite a lot actually.

Horror stories from a number of retailers abound of how they failed their customers in the run up to Christmas. Delivering Christmas fayre on the 26th OK? Sorry – we'll let you have a voucher with our apologies. On the one hand this is simply not good enough but on the other it is a sign of a creaking supply chain which simply cannot keep up with the ever-increasing demands consumers are placing on retailers. Maybe it's time to take stock and ask where the real value lies. What is it that shoppers really want from retailers? Is it low prices? Is it 24/7 availability? Is it a great experience? One thing's for sure; if consumers want it all, it will come at a price. The question is - are shoppers ready to pay that price?

M&S Sells Great Food, But Simply Dull Clothes

First published in Retail Week 18 October 2016

It seems like forever that Marks & Spencer has experienced very different fortunes according to which business one looks at. Food is a well-respected, liked and a trusted brand for many reasons while clothing – well, where do we begin?

In September, M&S revealed a restructuring of its London head office, which will result in the loss of over 500 jobs. Chief executive Steve Rowe was quoted as saying: "We have to become a simpler and more effective organisation if we are to deliver our plans to recover and grow our business." But is that going far enough?

Sales figures from both M&S and John Lewis are revealing – in the 13 weeks to July M&S achieved a 4% increase in food sales, but there was an 8.3% fall in clothing and home. In the first half to July, John Lewis generated a 2.2% increase at Waitrose and a 4.5% rise at John Lewis. The answer is not straightforward and lies in a number of aspects of the offering. We know that alarm bells have been ringing for many a year, but the thorny problem of clothing won't go away. So, what are the key areas in need of addressing?

Product

For years M&S was at least famous for something: underwear. However, recently even that has struggled to shine, surrounded by dull and uninspiring ranges – although cashmere is typically an oasis.

Merchandising

Poor product poorly merchandised is a recipe for disaster and yet M&S has been wedded to the same format for years. Even Per Una looks decidedly tired these days.

Stores

Unlike the food business, M&S clothing is saddled with a tired and under-invested estate. Where food stores have a clear and unequivocal brand, clothing by comparison is dull dreary and hard to understand. This is not an easy nut to crack but crack it he must if Steve Rowe is to rebuild a successful fashion business.

Competition

As the M&S offering has largely stood still, the competition has intensified in terms of price, product and experience. Indeed, the challenge is now not simply to catch up, but to take a quantum leap. The opportunity to achieve this extremely difficult feat appears to be rapidly dwindling. All of the above adds up to M&S losing the trust of its customers in its (clothing) brand and it is becoming less and less relevant. As the competition seeks ever-more innovative ways to excite and entice us on our individual journeys, M&S remains static and mired in an ageing demographic. There are some clear lessons from Bhs and Austin Reed to be learned, but whether it is too late for M&S remains to be seen. After all, the cashmere oasis can only provide so much sustenance.

What Women Want And Why You Should Pay Attention To Them

First published in Forbes 27 December 2018

I'm going to let you in on a secret; men and women are wired differently. Seriously, I know, I'm married to one! You just might be too. Now, you might be thinking that I'm targeting a male-only audience, and you'd be right; because women already know what's coming next.

OK, so we all know that us men can't control our egos whilst women have a monopoly on intuition. But that doesn't appear to be recognized in retail boardrooms up and down the country. I often feel like saying; 'what if you combined the best of both those characteristics, how much more successful would you be?'

But rather than concerning ourselves with diversity for the moment, let's consider that what women want from a retailer should be of utmost interest to every retail CEO, male or female. Here's why.

According to a recent poll conducted by Green Room Design, every respondent either strongly or mostly agreed that human experiences based on feminine insights can elevate the retail journey for everyone. This is important; because more and more, we are seeking more immersive, more connected and more engaging retail experiences. No longer are we prepared to accept mediocre because we know that the experience can be so much better. And we are quick to go in search of that better, more human experience. And it is women who are largely driving this. Catherine Lucas, Managing Partner at Green Room Design, believes that 'women want the same as men - the opportunity and the feeling that they've been considered; that they matter just as much'.

Leave egos at the door

Matter they do; Catalyst.org estimates that in the U.K. 67% of all household consumption is controlled or influenced by women. Brands are getting smarter and realizing that it's to women that they need to focus their attention. We all know the familiar cry from men who just 'hate shopping' and if we are ever coerced into partaking of this strange activity, we do so begrudgingly but with a sense of purpose. Get in, get out as quickly as possible. Military style operation, no dwell time, no browsing; simply execute the plan.

Women on the other hand shop with all their senses. Touch, smell, sight, hearing, taste - and probably a sixth too. This has implications. Not only that, according to consumer psychologists, empathy, relevance, warmth & inclusiveness all feature highly on women's priorities. I recently visited a Lululemon store in Covent

Garden in London, on entering, the first thing which I immediately noticed was the very pleasant aroma. There and then, my hand might have dug just a little deeper into my pocket. Now, aromatic diffusers a wonderful retail experience don't maketh on their own, but what they do is help create an environment conducive to not only spending time but also spending money. Take the diffuser a little further, and all of a sudden, a magical space is created where humans want to linger and socialize, just for the pleasure they derive from it. And in doing so, they are drawn ever closer to your brand.

As we move into the New Year, expect to see more and more of these inspiring retail spaces and remember that women have had a significant influence on their creation. Because in retail, egos amount to nothing and should be left at the door, whereas intuition is the guiding star.

You May Have Won My Mind, Amazon, But Not My Heart

First published in Forbes 3 June 2019

Ever wondered why you shop where you shop? I have. And every time I come to the same conclusion: it's either convenient or it inspires me. Which is why I am an Amazon Prime customer. It just works. Simple, efficient, dependable. Like a Honda. Or a Labrador. But does it inspire me? No. Not at all. Because to inspire means to excite and engage in some kind of relationship, and there's the thing. Amazon doesn't do relationships. It hasn't got time, it's far too busy disrupting the next sector, throwing the rulebook out of the window, experimenting with new concepts, and for what reason? Well, because it can.

Which brings me to the new "Clicks & Mortar" pop-up opened in Manchester today, launched in conjunction with the small business support organization Enterprise Nation. The shop sells everything from food and drink to electronics, beauty products, and homewares, as well as offering handy Amazon Lockers for customers to collect their (Amazon) orders. Amazon plans to open just ten such shops, much like supermarket chain Tesco, which currently has plans to open around a dozen of its new format Jack's discount stores. And that begs the question, why bother? But that would be to miss the point of the venture which we can be sure will be carefully monitored. The ten stores are part of a pilot to provide small online businesses with their first taste of having a physical presence. You'd be forgiven for a raised eyebrow.

Amazon, responsible—in part—for the struggle our high streets are now facing, and paying the same in corporation tax as department store Debenhams pay on their London's Oxford Street store alone, is supporting small online businesses to get a foothold on the high street. Search for "irony" on Amazon's website and the search results include a leather belt and a child's pushchair. So, I asked Alexa, and she replied, "humorously sarcastic or mocking." Now, I doubt that Amazon set out to do either of these things with the opening of Clicks & Mortar but still there remains that nagging feeling.

Just like the good people of the town of Lago in the Clint Eastwood spaghetti western *High Plains Drifter,* should we fear or welcome the "stranger"? For all those businesses seemingly benefiting now from having a physical presence, are they selling their souls or are they the smart ones? Doug Gurr, Amazon U.K.'s country manager, said: "Amazon is committed to supporting the growth of small businesses, helping them boost the economy and create jobs across the U.K. Small businesses are one of our most important customer groups." Emma Jones, the founder of Enterprise Nation, said: "U.K. shoppers like to shop both online and in high street stores [and this will] enable customers to discover new brands on their local high streets." All very laudable and to be applauded.

But spiralling business rates have hit the high street hard. According to *The Guardian*, this year Amazon confirmed that it pays business rates of just £63.4 million—almost £40 million less than fashion and home retailer Next, despite sales of more than double the U.K. company. In this context, the sentiment from Amazon seems somewhat incongruous. But that won't deter the large majority of us. After all, we're in love with ease and convenience, it's just that Amazon does it rather better than anyone else. Who said anything about the death of the high street?

Calling Julian Dunkerton At Superdry, You're No Longer In Fashion

First published in Forbes 10 July 2019

Now, I don't know about you but I've never been one to be all shouty about the clothes I'm wearing. The thought of having the brand emblazoned across my chest has never been that attractive a proposition. Seems I'm not alone. Because a generation who grew up wearing the "Japanese" branded Superdry clothing (of course, we know it was born in Cheltenham) — and feeling ultra-cool in doing so — are now deserting it in their droves.

From profits of £65.3 million to a pre-tax loss of £85.4 million announced earlier today, for the once super trendy brand, best known for its jackets and hoodies, the harsh reality of the new consumer-driven world of fashion has come as a sharp shock. Shares dropped more than 4% on Wednesday as the City digested the news. The boardroom travails at Superdry are well known, resulting in the mass exodus of previous chief executive Euan Sutherland and his team, to be replaced by the returning founder of the business Julian Dunkerton, in April this year.

Using a tried and tested retail strategy of being publicly scathing of the previous management team, Dunkerton has a huge task on his hands to restore the brand to the position on the high street it, until recently, enjoyed. Because, even in the time since March 2018 when Dunkerton left the business, the pace of change and consumer demands in the fashion world have been nothing if not rapid. Which begs the question of not when but if he can restore success to the brand. And building on that style for any new retail chief executive, he claims that performance in the new financial year will "reflect market conditions and the (historical) issues inherited." In other words, performance is likely to fall still further.

"The issues in the business will not be resolved overnight," Dunkerton said. "Although we are only three months in, our initiatives are gaining some early traction and I am confident we are doing the right things to ensure that over time Superdry will return to strong profitable growth."

The Problem For Superdry

I decided to put that claim to the ultimate test today by asking a group of (mainly female) teenagers I met in London what they thought of Superdry. The responses were revealing, and in some cases, surprising. Much of what they said bore out my initial suspicions that the typical Superdry customer has simply moved on to find alternative brands. Why? Because they got fed up wearing clothes their whole family was also wearing. This is a key issue for Superdry. After all, which self-respecting teenager is going to be seen wearing the same gear as their parents? In order to succeed then, Dunkerton is going to have to restore a large dollop of street-cred to the brand and have a laser-sharp focus on who the Superdry customer really is. But that's not all. According to the teenagers I spoke to, Superdry has become a "bit like Hollister." In other words, a brand which was once trendy but has now become a bit long in the tooth.

But the real surprise came when I asked the group where they prefer to shop. As expected, ASOS featured "because there's always something new to try" along with Urban Outfitters and the creative social shopping app Depop. But the list contained one other which came as a surprise: Topshop. Contrary to received wisdom for many, according to the group I spoke to, Topshop remains one of their go-to destinations for today's fashion wear, for girls at least. Which rather means that a revival of Superdry is not entirely out of the question. The only thing is, it just has to stock product that doesn't appeal to Mums and Dads.

Forget Customer Experience, Boris Johnson Will See To That

First published in Forbes 21 July 2019

Hard though it is to imagine these days, but mankind wasn't born to operate an iPhone. Or order an Uber. Or a takeaway at just the touch of a few icons. No, we were born hunter gatherers, and the only takeaway we would bring home still had its horns intact and wasn't in a particularly good mood.

You see, back in the days when we had to light a fire to keep our caves lit, life was a little simpler. No irritating customer satisfaction surveys to litter our inbox. "How did you find catching armadillo today? Was it a) a walk in the tundra, b) a walk on the wild side, or c) a walk too far. Neither did we have to worry ourselves too much with the nuances of the experience itself. "Welcome home dear, how was your day? Did you have a wonderful customer experience chasing wildebeest? Don't worry, you'll get to bop one over the head next time."

No, in those days, the supply chain was a little more straightforward and we really didn't bother with quite how we did our "shopping." Fast forward to 2007 and Steve Jobs put paid to all that. Because when he got up on stage at Macworld in January of that year, he launched onto an unsuspecting world, what was the equivalent of our ancestors' lump of wood, something with which to beat over the head any passing antelope. Except that this lump of wood held magic powers, powers we previously could only have dreamed of possessing. Because in the smartphone we suddenly had a voice, and we soon discovered that we could exert power and influence over our prey. And overnight, customer experience was born.

An Entire Industry

Today, an entire customer experience industry has evolved. Bringing with it new terms such as the wonderfully awful "experiential" retail. Nowadays it seems that the experience is more important than the quality of the product or the price for that matter. Personally, I don't source my smartphones from Silicon Valley, but for those who do, it's more like a religion and if you've ever visited one of their temples, you'll see why Apple followers are so loyal. They go not just for the product but for the whole experience.

Everywhere we turn, we are asked for our feedback on our experience. It pervades virtually every interaction we have, whether it be flying, booking a holiday or using the bathroom. But that's all about to change because Boris Johnson will become prime minister and customer experience will suddenly be the last thing on our minds. Because in a post-Brexit no-deal Britain, we'll find ourselves resorting to our ancestors' ways of catching dinner. And all of a sudden, we will collectively find ourselves at the very bottom of Maslow. And at the same time, the whole concept of customer experience will become but a distant memory. "How was your experience of trying to find a pint of milk?" "Well, actually I'm just glad I found one come to think of it."

According to Government figures, in 2017, U.K. exports to the EU were £274 billion (44% of all U.K. exports). U.K. imports from the EU were £341 billion (53% of all U.K. imports). And what's more, almost 30% of our food comes from the EU. In a no-deal Brexit, those irritating trade agreements will be thrown into something resembling a teenager's rave party. Which is unfortunate, as it's really rather going to mess things up. Just think, the French will suddenly control the consumption of your favourite Roquefort. And in that scenario, you really won't care about how nicely it's presented or the length of the queue at the checkout.

PART TWO: I AM THEREFORE I SHOP

We all need to shop, it's just that we are doing so in different ways now. We are far removed from the behaviour of our parents and this has caught out many on the High Street who are still stuck in the past.

Previously we looked at our expectations as consumers and how these are influencing our shopping behaviour and whilst it is true that the uncertainty surrounding our future as a member of the European Union is having an impact on consumer confidence, we are still shopping. And we will continue to need to shop. Discretionary items such as that new three-piece suite, or that new super fifty-inch TV may have to wait a little longer but fundamentally we continue to spend, to consume.

It's just that what we seek in terms of our shopping experience has changed out of all recognition. We have been educated to expect cheap clothes and cheap food, we have been educated to expect to be able to buy an avocado all year round. It wasn't that long ago that you couldn't buy an avocado at all. More travel has led to more of us acquiring new tastes and therefore expectations of grocery shopping. Fast fashion gets a bad press right now and perhaps this is understandable as we all become more aware of the planet, climate change and the legacy we will leave for future generations. Sustainability has become the word of the decade. But still we expect to be able to grab that £5 T-shirt to take on holiday and more often than that, return without it.

Personalisation and customer experience

Much is written about personalisation and customer experience – the two are natural bedfellows - and if we believe much of what we read, we would be forgiven for thinking that both are highly sophisticated and mature. That both are the product of much development and investment, consequently delivering that most elusive of factors – customer 'stickability' or as some would have it – loyalty. Because whatever our shopping journey, we expect both in abundance. After all, are there any of us who don't like to be made a little special? Provided it is done in an unobtrusive, respectful manner.

In truth, whilst there's no doubting that retailers increasingly understand that they must make a significant commitment to both, the reality is very different. When Liam Fox was referring to British business as being 'fat and lazy' back in September 2016, he could so easily have been referring to personalisation and customer experience. Why? Current attempts at personalisation are both one dimensional and reactive, at best relying on calendar entries and smart mirrors to create an illusion of personalised engagement. As an example, I recently received (through my letterbox no less) a card from a well-known national florist, reminding me that it was my mother's birthday soon and suggesting which flower arrangement I may wish to send. I thanked them for their interest, informing them that my mother had passed away 9 months previously. Now, I hear you ask; how on earth are they expected to know that my mother had passed away? My response – don't be lazy, true personalisation is knowing your customer and engaging in a relevant, contextual manner. Not simply relying on calendar prompts and firing off unsolicited mailshots. Show me that you can engage in a relevant manner and I will happily provide the information necessary to give you the context.

Simple tracking of social media can provide deep insights into many different aspects of our lives – how we are feeling, if we are on holiday, our interests, our priorities even what mood we are in. And what's more, as consumers, many of us are willing to pay for what in reality we should expect as the new normal. According to Deloitte in a report published in 2015 titled "The Rise of Mass Personalisation", one in five consumers who expressed an interest in personalised products or services are willing to pay a 20% premium. So, what does all this mean? The implications for retailers who do not embrace the technology required to deliver a personalised experience for their customers are clear and serious. Never before have we, as consumers, been so demanding, so promiscuous – willing to drop a brand and move to the competition without hesitation. And what's more, our expectations keep on growing exponentially. Only those retailers who understand this will survive, the outlook for the remainder is bleak.

And much of this is a generational thing, I'm referring of course to millennials and to generation Z – the latter being those born since 1995. They grew up never knowing a pre-9/11 world, the age of austerity was just normal to them as they had never known anything any different. But that's not all. Imagine being freaked out by an internet dial-up tone or wondering what a landline signal is? Or how about not knowing a world without the internet or the smartphone? Give them a cassette and a pencil and they'd have no idea what the pencil is for. Sadly, many of us can remember exactly what it was for!

Anything which came before is in the past, they can only relate to it by reading about it; not through their own experience and memory of it. Why are they significant for retailers? They're already the most influential group of technology trendsetters and they offer the best preview of future trends, such as technology usage, communication, banking, and shopping patterns. True digital natives, for them there is no such thing as a work / life balance; it's just a work / life blend and it is ongoing 24 / 7. You see, for them, the concept of the workplace is different too; anywhere they are online is the workplace.

Previously I suggested that all of us, the consumer, is the most disruptive force in retail and the most disruptive cohort of all is generation Z. Driving a pace of change previously unheard of, they are re-writing the rule book. For them, technology isn't driving the experience, technology IS the experience. It is for this reason why so many retail brands are failing: they are run by Generation X and Baby Boomers whose judgements and decisions are informed by their own perception of the world, in turn informed by their own experiences. According to Jason Dorsey, President of the Centre For Generational Kinetics based in Austin, Texas, technology is only new if you remember it the way it was before. For generation Z they don't have this memory to view technology in a completely different way. And it would be a grave mistake to think of generation Z as teenagers and twentysomethings with no real spending power or influence. Here's the thing: the greatest predictor of the behaviour of older generations is found in what generation Z are doing today. Ignore them at your peril because generation Z don't see your business the way you do.

With an estimated 2.6 billion members globally, they expect to be able to engage with your brand – and you with them, and what's more, they even want to get involved in your product design! The truth is that they are redefining the very relationship, the very nature of what it means to shop. And with it, the relationship we have with brands. Being the first true digital native generation, as mentioned before, they have never known a world without the internet, therefore their attitudes towards technology are fundamentally different to those of the rest of us. I've always concluded that if you explained to any retail CEO how a teenager uses their smartphone and interacts (with brands, friends etc.) with it, they would understand what you mean on an intellectual level, because they are smart people. But and this is a very big but, for the average fifty something retail CEO, they would never understand what you meant on an emotional level. Therefore, they would never truly, instinctively understand the importance of certain investment decisions for their business. This mismatch between those running retail businesses and a large proportion of their customer base is in large part why we are seeing many of the legacy retailers who began as a physical entity and then had to move online (with the notable exception of Primark) beginning to struggle.

This is very important when you consider brand experience; why? Because generation Z don't recognise 'omnichannel' - a term largely coined by baby boomers incidentally – it's all simply one brand entity which might be accessed one moment via a mobile device and the next by entering your store. To them there is no difference. One thing however is clear: generation Z are far less tolerant of any technical glitches than any other group. That's because technology isn't considered something special, it is not an adjunct to the 'digital experience', it IS the experience. But here's the apparent contradiction for retailers. In 2018 the National Retail Federation and IBM's Institute for Business Value conducted research and surveyed over 15,000 consumers aged 13-21 from 16 different countries. The results may come as something of a surprise. It found that this group - born into a world of digital devices and who love mobile - almost universally still prefer to shop in-store – all 96% of them! What does this mean for brands?

And therein lies the key to unlocking generation Z; whilst beneath the waves everything might be frantically working to keep the ship afloat be sure that above, all appears calm and serene. Technology in perfect harmony with the brand, choreographed elegantly such that the entire experience is seamless. Elsewhere in this book, we'll explore the impact and consequences of not maintaining and updating stores sufficiently. For it's not limited to generation Z.

The Human Touch Is Central To Brand Experience

First published in Retail Week 6 August 2014

Retail is a fascinating sector to be involved in and for me it's a passion. Why? We're a nation of shoppers and equally we're all consumers. So, it follows that unlike other sectors, we all have an attachment with retail brands, often on an emotional level, to a degree that we would never contemplate if it were, say banking, telecoms or utilities. Many column inches have been devoted of late to the dilemma facing Tesco and the challenge placed upon Dave Lewis when he takes the reins from Philip Clarke in October. I don't wish to add to those here except to say that I for one will be watching closely. Tesco will survive, of that there is no doubt, but in what guise the brand will develop in years to come will be an endless source of interest.

Tesco is not unique in having a brand problem and it is the link between brand perception and customer experience that interests. The type of experience a retailer delivers to its customers is intrinsically linked to the way the brand is perceived and therefore the level of loyalty it enjoys. We all know what we think of whenever brands such as Apple, Burberry or Waitrose are mentioned so, surely, we know what every retailer stands for? They all market, advertise, entice us to buy - so we would know, wouldn't we? Wrong.

The successful brands understand not the what but the why. Why are they in business? Why should consumers shop with them? Why do they behave the way they do? They understand what they stand for. They also engage with their customers like never before. They have realised the importance of interaction on all levels and know that just one negative experience can alienate a customer for good. And while much of the enabler for this engagement is driven through innovative use of technology, the face of the brand – its people - can make or break all the technology in the world. I was reminded of this when in my local Boots the other day shopping for sun cream for a forthcoming holiday.

After fruitlessly scouring the first few aisles without success and looking for appropriate signage (which I expected to be prominent at this time of year) I did what comes as alien behaviour to all men; I asked for directions. And it was this interaction which was revealing. I found the nearest on-floor store colleague and asked if I could be pointed in the direction of the sun creams, to be told in a somewhat terse, almost condescending way "you're looking at them". All the technology in the world can transform a brand but one negative human interaction will undo all that in a heartbeat.

Is Your Retail Model Set Up For Baby Boomers, Not Millennials?

First published in Retail Week, 21 October 2014

Bold, brash, impatient, demanding… the millennial is a new breed of customer. One who doesn't conform, isn't loyal, wants everything now and ultimately could destroy your brand if they don't get what they want. Excite, engage, explore, expand – or die. That's the message today and we hear the same or similar over and over but what is behind the race to digitise? For that is what is happening on a high street near you; it's a race like no other and if a favourite retail brand isn't part of it then it can be safely assumed, they may not be around much longer. If you are reading this and were born before 1970, you and I see the world from a similar perspective.

We grew up with no internet (how on earth did we get by?), no mobile phones (yes, we were tied to the length of the landline phone cable) and as for music, film, TV streaming - forget it, what was wrong with Betamax anyway? If, however, you were born after 1985, you are probably wondering what on earth the last paragraph was all about. Imagining a life without the internet must be pretty hard to do, let alone smartphones, Facebook, Twitter, Instagram, YouTube. How on earth did we share our lives before social media? We never socialised, never communicated, never engaged, never bothered to contact all those hundreds of (Facebook) friends we thought we knew?

Life and expectations in 2014 are light years away from even 10 years ago, let alone the 1980s and the pace of change is simply mind boggling. Who do those demanding millennials want to engage with most? Well, I'll give you a clue, it's not their favourite utility company or their favourite bank; no, it's with their favourite retail brand(s). Why? Because, retail represents a large part of how they affirm their lifestyle, how they affirm themselves, indeed… ultimately how they perceive their place in the world. Seems exaggerated? Farfetched? Well, consider your own teenage children for just a moment and you will quickly come to an amazing conclusion. Whether it be clothes, gym membership, jewellery, make and model of smartphone, network, gaming prowess - the list goes on – there are a large number of critical, life-affirming dynamics which in the digital world are of complete and total importance and relevance to the millennial living with you.

Most existing retail business models are built on a 1970s baby boomer perception of a parent child relationship with their customers. That no longer applies; that millennial upstairs has wildly different and perverse expectations of not only the world around them but of their favourite brands. They expect to get what they want, when and where they want it. But scarily and all too frequently ignored by the typical corporate attitude of today, they expect to see a real cause and effect when engaging with brands.

To be able to influence, whether it be product, price, place, marketing – the list goes on - they expect to be able to be an integral part of the product development and not only that but to be rewarded for their input. Yes, you read that correctly. Millennials expect to be rewarded for their input. The retail business model as we know it is dead. The really intriguing question is who are the ones who realise this?

Five Reasons Why The Department Store Model Is Far From Dead

First published in Forbes, 3 November 2018

"The report of my death was an exaggeration" that oft-misquoted line from Mark Twain when on a trip to London in 1897 after rumours starting spreading of his grave ill-health then death. Just twelve years later, in 1909, Harry Selfridge opened his eponymous store on Oxford Street in London. In so many ways he was far ahead of his time and it is a testament to his foresight that we can still learn much from him today. Treat [the customer] as guests when they come and when they go, whether or not they buy. Give them all that can be given fairly, on the principle that 'to him that giveth shall be given'. Harry Gordon Selfridge

Harry Selfridge had an underlying philosophy that his store shouldn't be seen simply as a 'shop' where he sold 'stuff'. He was passionate about Selfridges being a social and cultural centre, one where people could commune, relax, browse - enjoy the experience. Strangely, the very same values and qualities we place on great customer experience today, over a hundred years later. The department store model is perfectly able to survive and in actuality, should be able to thrive in this e-commerce age but needs to display a number of characteristics in order to do so. Here are the top five:

Destination

For any department store to be successful, the very nature of it demands that it is a 'destination' for shoppers, somewhere to spend time rather than merely 'shopping'. If it doesn't do this, why bother to have a department store at all? The nature of most is that they are intrinsically large spaces, therefore this space should be used to create something inspiring rather than simply filling the space with product.

Stimulate the senses

I previously used a quotation from Boxpark founder, Roger Wade, when he was referring to online and never a truer word was spoken. In other words, if I'm coming to a department store, I am seeking a multi-sensory experience. One that will stay in my memory. To take an insight from psychology - the memory of the experience is more important than the experience itself.

Sprinkle a little fairy dust

Let's face it; life's hard enough as it is right? So why not provide a little magic, a little inspiration to keep us not only entertained but above all, curious. What's around the next corner? What will I find? The best do this in spades - and keep us coming back because they are constantly updating that experience.

Surprise me

The space which your average department store enjoys is both a handicap and an asset. Whilst the costs might be huge, the opportunity to continually use that space in more and more imaginative ways is an advantage, others do not enjoy. Whether it be a skate bowl as in Selfridges in London, the element of surprise to inspire and delight your customers should be second nature.

We're human after all

Above all, we're all human. Whether it be augmented reality, virtual reality, robots you name it there are a plethora of technology solutions out there. But above all, great retail relies on great human interaction. Humans first, technology second.

If executed well, the department store has a unique place in the retail landscape and offers something which no other retail formats can provide. "We see our physical stores as social hubs, as much as we do retail spaces - it's something which has been part of our DNA since the store opened in 1909. The introduction of a working skate bowl is a decision we arrived at early on" Bosse Myhr, Selfridges Director of Menswear. All those years ago, Harry Selfridge was way ahead of his time; and today he still provides the blueprint for the successful department store model.

Black Friday Blues: Is The Annual Orgy Of Excess Losing Its Appeal?

First published in Forbes 23 November 2018

What do Primark, B&Q, Asda, Fat Face, House of Fraser and Selfridges all have in common? Yes, that's right - they've all opted out of Black Friday; eschewing the opportunity to mark-down in favour of trading business as usual on one of the busiest trading days of the year.

It might lie in the shadow of Alibaba's Singles Day which topped $30 billion in 2018, (American consumers spent $19.62 billion during the Black Friday event in 2017), but Black Friday remains a global phenomenon. Here in the U.K. it appears that consumer appetite for a pre-Brexit bargain is undiminished although behaviour is changing with a 78% increase in online sales over last year before we had even reached 7am this morning. But then - and here's the thing - it's no longer Black Friday, it's Black Friday week. As life becomes tougher for retailers, they respond by going on sale for longer; just at a time when they least need to be. Trapped in a Black Friday conundrum, most find it hard not to resist the increased sales - at the risk of margin. Introduced to the U.K. by Amazon back in 2010, Black Friday went largely unnoticed; that is until 2013 when retailers such as Walmart owned Asda starting offering TVs at huge knockdown prices.

The result? Near riots in their stores as people wrestled with each other in order to grab a bargain. Asda no longer participates in Black Friday. On the face of it, Black Friday is good for consumers and good for retailers but not all agree. Veteran retail analyst Richard Hyman was moved to say: 'Black Friday has probably been the most stupid retail import this country has ever seen. To launch a promotion when you are wanting, and needing, to promote your Christmas ranges is very confusing for customers.'

Even some online fashion retailers are believed to be opting out this year. So, what's the problem? Have we fallen out of love with the discount event of the year? The truth is that whilst in the U.S. - following Thanksgiving as it does - it makes a lot more sense. In the U.K. the focus has always been about the run up to Christmas and the bargains that can be found during that period and the traditional Boxing Day sales. To introduce an artificial discount event such as Black Friday in effect upsets the entire retail ecosystem, makes life very challenging for retailers and confuses customers. According to research by consumer group Which? most products are actually cheaper at other times of the year.

For fashion retailers, in particular, Black Friday is a massive headache, the volume of returns causing major problems for their supply chains. But the annual frenzy continues unabated, seduced by offers of up to 50%, even 70% off in some cases, it appears that we all like to feel we've grabbed ourselves a bargain. But as always, we must wait for those returns to be calculated before assessing the true performance of this Black Friday. After all, a bargain's only a bargain if we needed it in the first place.

Massive, Fun and Cheap. Why The New Primark Store In Birmingham Is Sure To Succeed

First published in Forbes 12 April 2019

Located on the site of the old Pavilions Shopping Centre, the new Primark store, which opened in Birmingham yesterday, covers 161,000 square feet over five floors and is the biggest in the world. On entering the store you are greeted with the welcome "Hello Brum.....Find Your Amazing". And amazing it most certainly is. A huge monument to fast fashion, bringing rock bottom affordable prices to the masses. There is quite simply nowhere else like it. Unless you visit Primark Manchester. Or Primark Madrid for that matter.

An anticipated 5,000 people were expected to visit the store on opening day and it felt as if all 5,000 were there when I visited during the afternoon. Clutching huge baskets, brimming with garments, it was clear that the good people of Birmingham couldn't wait for this day to come.

Primark famously eschews the online world (although at the time of writing there are suggestions that they are considering an online presence) and this writer for one applauds their staunch belief in the store-based shopping experience. This new Birmingham store is evidence not only that stores are far from dead, department stores - if done well - have a great future. For this is in effect what this is - a department store. And while others flounder and lose their way, Primark has shown us what good looks like. From the Disney themed restaurant, to the barbers, to the beauty salon to the custom lab, the store manages to pull off that somewhat elusive trick. That of providing something new and unexpected around just about every corner.

It's about giving people what they want and the reality is that for many of us, many fashion retailers are just too expensive but equally, we want to be able to buy ourselves new clothes. While this might be experiential retail on steroids, affordability is what Primark does best. Famous for low prices - Primark's doesn't really do advertising - it's needed to maintain this in the face of some fierce criticism of its environmental commitments over recent years, leaving the brand open to the question whether their low prices are at the expense of the environment? They are a member of the sustainable apparel coalition and have signed the Bangladesh Accord and Cotton Pledge amongst other initiatives but according Good On You, which rates brands' ethical credentials, Primark has a way to go yet. But that aside, they are very adept and laser-focused on one thing: giving the customer what they want, in a fun and enticing way.

Retail analyst Kate Hardcastle, from Insight with Passion, said people "foolishly" looked at Primark as a discount brand. "It is anything but," she said. "They are savvy, they know what they are doing. The easiest way to describe the department shops of old was they were too lazy, they stopped putting the customer and changing demands at the heart of their vision. They very much took footfall for granted, they always thought if they opened their doors, people would come. Primark understands what customers want and built their business around it."

And in that analysis, we discover the core of why some are struggling where Primark are succeeding: putting the customer at the very heart of their business, giving them what they want, and in particular being famous for something. OK so not everything was on point on opening day, the WiFi wasn't great and the lights briefly went out but these are minor glitches. Because Primark, perhaps more than any other high street retailer, is very clear about what its brand stands for. No fuss, no tinkering, no misleading, just clear, honest to goodness retailing. The department store is dead, long live the department store.

Shoppers Secretly Being Filmed The Shocking Truth Behind Retailers Tricking Us Into Buying More

First published in Forbes 24 April 2019

Boots, Asda, Tesco, B&Q, Co-op - they've all admitted to doing it but is it a serious breach of our personal privacy? I'm talking about secretly filming us while we shop in order to influence our behaviour and trick us into buying more. Really? Well, true but only if you believed the sensationalist headlines that screamed out from the pages of the likes of the *Daily Mail* and *Metro* newspapers yesterday. If like me, you read them with a growing sense of incredulity you'd probably agree that in reality, the truth is rather different. And here's why.

Consider the clickbait headlines just for a moment and it's not difficult to see that they are complete nonsense. Sadly, many never get past the headline (hopefully though you've got this far!). The main thrust of the story was that retailers, such as those named above, who, by the way, are guilty of nothing whatsoever, had used the services of a firm called Shopping Behaviour Xplained (SBXL) who are specialists in identifying our habits and behaviours when we are out shopping.

Using secret (but with customer consent through clear signage) filming they are able to properly observe the ways that we navigate a store, where we dwell, how much time we spend, our consciousness of signage, and so forth. The only thing they did incorrectly was to then post the footage on social media. The key to this, of course, is to be able to observe and record our natural shopping behaviours, if we thought we were on camera then our actions would most likely be artificial and entirely misleading. In his excellent book Consumer.ology, Philip Graves explains this phenomenon and how most market research techniques are fundamentally flawed. Because in a staged environment, such as when interviewing consumers for market research we tend to give the answers that we think the interviewer wants from us, as opposed to our true feelings and future intentions. So that helps to explain why secret filming is required in order to accurately capture our shopping behaviour but of course, if you believed the headlines, the long and disturbing shadow of an Orwellian society is cast. Secretly being filmed - should we care?

Walk down any high street, drive on any motorway, visit a restaurant, a football stadium, a hotel, a bar - practically everywhere we go these days we are on CCTV. And no-one bats an eyelid. So 'secret' filming is nothing new, in fact, it's now an accepted part of our everyday lives. As for "controlling emotions and behaviour" as the story in the *Daily Mail* claims, well, that's where it gets quite interesting. As emotions play a major role in our lives, this of course means that consumers' decisions are less logical and more emotional. And it is to consumer and behavioural psychologists that we need to turn in order to uncover whether that is a valid claim.

In her excellent blog "Inside the mind of the consumer", Zana Busby explores the role our emotions play in our shopping behaviour. And we might be shocked to learn that around 80% of our decision making is made on an emotional level by our sub-conscious mind. In effect, when we enter a supermarket, for instance, we are on auto-pilot. Therefore, it makes perfect sense for retailers to try to better understand our behaviour when we are out shopping if only to provide a better offer to us. And in this era of customer experience and experiential retail, surely that can only be a good thing?

The Shop Now, Pay Later Model Is Gaining Popularity: Here's Why

First published in Forbes 17 June 2019

You know the feeling; you want—no, you've convinced yourself that you *need*, that new pair of jeans. The only trouble is, they're selling at a pretty hefty £99 and there's the small matter of the rent to pay. And buying food. And paying for the train ticket to work. Ah, well, save for another few months and might be able to get them then. Except that things are rapidly changing in the world of payments. With more and more of the younger generation (think millennial) either unable or unwilling to have a credit card, this has given rise to the era of "buy now, pay later." Once associated with having a bit of a stigma, it is quickly changing the whole way that we shop.

And at the forefront of this are <u>Klarna</u>. Founded in Stockholm in 2005, they entered the U.K. market in 2014 and now partner with over 130,000 retailers globally, including Arcadia Group, ASOS, JD sports, Mothercare, Gymshark, Missguided, Swoon, and Samsung. They claim to provide an alternative payment method which gives consumers options to pay after they have received the goods or in fixed payments, entirely interest and fee free. No wonder it's catching on. Last week they opened a pop-up shop in the centre of London; this was a physical store with a selection of their online retail partners. I spoke to their CEO Sebastian Siematowski, about Klarna and about the pop-up shop.

The thinking behind the concept is one of "responsible lending" he said, adding that "it has to be super easy. Using Klarna should be easier than using your card." In the U.K., this means purchasing an item and paying for it either 30 days later or spreading payments over three months in equal amounts. Siematowski showed me the Klarna app and some of the features soon to be introduced, including being able to easily track your spending. Interestingly, Siematowski realized that Klarna was becoming large and in doing so becoming more and more bureaucratic. His answer to this was to create teams across the business and then empower them. To date, there are over 200 of these teams all operating like internal startups.

One of them came up with the idea of the pop-up as a means to bring awareness not just of Klarna but of their previously purely online digital retail partners. For some of whom, this was their first foray into the world of physical retail. One such was Charlotte O'Reilly, owner of Charlotte Jade, producers of hand-drawn, interior patterns inspired by nature. These are then transformed into wallpapers, textiles, soft furnishings, furniture, ceramic tiles, and other interior designs. At over a hundred pounds for just one roll of wallpaper, these are a far cry from picking up half a dozen rolls at your local B&Q. She was delighted with the pop-up, saying that it allowed her to show her brand in ways that simply aren't possible online. "It's very much a case of facilitating experiences and growing awareness," she added.

I asked Siematowski about the future for Klarna. "Returns is becoming a big challenge for retailers and of course we have the data, so I see that as an area for further development," he said. Apparently, Klarna is a Swedish word meaning "clarity," it's not yet in the Oxford English dictionary but it can't be long before a new verb will be found there, "to Klarna it," meaning the act of using pay later at your favourite retailer.

PART THREE: CUSTOMER FIRST, NO REALLY

There's not a retailer who would disagree with always putting the customer first and that they put the customer at the heart of their operations. But how many *really* live and breathe this? Most in reality pay lip service to this and think that mediocre can be acceptable. Here's why.

Talk to an independent retailer or a new start-up and it becomes very clear, very soon that they have a laser focus on the customer. This is no coincidence. Independent retailers tend to be smaller, perhaps one or two stores or an online presence still requiring them to personally pack the product ready for shipping. They simply cannot *afford* to take their eye off the customer. Everything they do is geared around satisfying the customer and delivering excellence at all times. Contrast this with what I refer to as 'legacy' retailers, the chains we all know so well, those who have been in existence, perhaps for decades.

They most probably began life long before this thing we call the internet, ever was envisaged. Long before email, long before smartphones, long before VHS. Think about that for a moment. These retail businesses can often pre-date all of these things by many, many years. In an age even pre-dating barcodes and electronic point of sale, life was very different. And this meant that these businesses evolved in a very different way to those of today. The organisational structure was characterised by a vertical, top down, command and control mentality. The centre, comprising all its requisite departments, logistics, commercial, merchandising, buying, marketing and so forth, supported by HR, finance and IT, dictated to the stores. Compliance and governance were the watchwords. The company ran itself for the good of the business and its shareholders. They stocked stores with product and expected us to walk in and purchase. And repeat. Added to which, retailers not only dictated to their store operations, they dictated to us, their customers. Their business was run to strict metrics designed to monitor and measure direct sales. Metrics such as footfall, basket size, sales per square foot and so on were developed and reported every Monday morning in the weekly sales meeting. All perfectly logical.

Fast forward to today and the entire landscape looks very different, especially the relationship retailers have with their customers. No longer accepting of what we are offered, we are now the ones who dictate by exercising not only choice but, through social media, we have found our voice. And we expect to be listened to. The only problem is, many retail businesses are still stuck in the old ways of working, unable or unwilling to change. Whilst the world has changed beyond recognition around them, they remain firmly in the last century. And in doing so they have not only lost customers, they have lost their relevance. These are the ones we see struggling today.

Are they structured and organised around the customer? Absolutely not. Their marketing messages belie the real truth. In an increasing number of cases they appoint a chief customer officer, as if this will cure the problem. But this only highlights the fact that they are unclear as to who 'owns' the customer relationship. Awash with more data than they can manage, they should know so much about us but in reality, it's very little. It's no coincidence that the likes of Topshop owners Arcadia, Debenhams, House of Fraser, Mothercare and many others are struggling to keep up. In the case of Arcadia, run as it is by Sir Philip Green, famous for retaining an old Nokia phone and not using email, it is easy to see why they have struggled to keep pace with the demands of today's ecommerce world. The investments needed to have been made ten years ago. I for one would not have relished trying to persuade him to part with £ millions to upgrade an aging eCommerce platform and logistics operation.

Putting the customer first is, of course, more than just a few catchy words in the company mission statement. It means putting them at the heart of everything the organisation does. Timpson is a retail business I have long admired, not least for taking ex-prisoners and giving them a new lease of life. They put the customer first by empowering their front-line staff. If a problem needs solving, they are empowered to the tune of £500 in order to solve it. Whatever is the right thing to do for the customer. That's powerful.

Much is talked about the customer journey but again, as in putting the customer first, how many live and breathe this? Back in the late nineties, I worked at Superdrug; if there's a better place to learn your retail trade, I've yet to find it. One of the things I still remember was something known as the 'double buggy test'. This literally entailed navigating a double buggy (double in terms of width) around the store. If this was not possible then the store would be reorganised in order for mothers with two small children to be able to get around the store. I would go even further. If you truly put the customer first, why not begin that physical journey at the train station, the bus stations, the car park? Now, the journey from any of these places isn't in the control, not even influence, of the retailer in the majority of cases but it would certainly provide a valuable insight into how your customer is *feeling* when they enter your store.

Why retail businesses fail

Life for retailers has never been tougher but being completely customer focused is within the grasp of every single one. To choose not to tread this path is baffling. Perhaps some of it is down to the short-term nature of the majority of retail businesses, after all, shareholders and private equity investors are not renowned for their patience. In September 2018, that bellwether of the high street, John Lewis posted its half year results which showed a 99% drop in pre-tax profits. But this was not met by the usual cacophony in the media because, as we know, it has a unique partner model

- being owned by all its staff – which means that it is always playing the long game. This is not the case for the majority. Not so long ago, American Eagle announced that after only three years it was pulling out of the UK market. Add to that the names of those who have exited or are struggling - J.Crew, American Apparel, Forever 21, Hollister and Banana Republic immediately come to mind - and you begin to see a trend appearing. What's behind this? Why are these brands failing? On the face of it, all should be performing well. Good stores, good locations and in most cases good customer experience. However, look a little closer and a different picture emerges.

Take American Eagle; three stores one in each of Westfield Stratford and Westfield Shepherds Bush and one in Bluewater. Those sites don't come cheap. Add to that the market they are in; attracting 15 to 25 year-olds with an affordable 'preppy' look – an age group notoriously fickle when it comes to fashion preferences. Oh, and add in the small matter of fast fashion icons such as H&M and Zara and it makes for a strong headwind. Put all that in the context of a decidedly challenging UK retail fashion landscape where, faced with rising costs and a slowdown in consumer spending, as we know, many of the more well-established retailers are struggling.

But for me there's another, perhaps more vital ingredient which is lacking. More than ever, brands are having to compete like crazy to get into our consciousness. According to research firm PMR, "the recall of one brand blocks off the other brands from the range of alternatives in which the consumer makes his/her selection". So, it's already extremely difficult to achieve any kind of brand awareness. But when one considers the penetration and influence which social media has today, the task of gaining brand recognition in a new market assumes almost herculean proportions.
In a recent blog from Brandwatch, up to "96% of conversations happen outside the official, owned channels of the brand". Therefore, it follows that the brand no longer owns the brand, the consumer does. Rather makes the case for being known for putting the customer first don't you think?

It's an intriguing proposition; does brand loyalty still exist? The effects of austerity continue to be felt and perhaps our shopping habits have changed forever.
I would argue that in order to be truly customer focused, a retailer must understand its why before anything else - why it is in business, and must be able to articulate that why in an effective manner. Unfortunately, too many continue to simply broadcast their message. In today's world of socially aware, savvy consumers, retailers also need to engage with their audience. It is about inspiring consumers; in his excellent book 'Start With Why', Simon Sinek says, "We are drawn to organisations that are good at communicating what they believe".

More than ever before, we need to understand what a retail brand stands for, why it is in business and what value it can offer us.

Toastie Wars!

First published in Retail Reflections 30 August 2017

In my job as a content writer I am fortunate enough to be able to work from virtually anywhere; provided I have my smartphone, laptop and decent WiFi I'm a happy camper. Today I have been working from home catching up on my accounts, planning a forthcoming speaking engagement, preparing for DMexco retail conference in Cologne in two weeks' time whilst also writing this blog. Over the last week I have been writing and speaking a fair amount on the subject of experience and expectation for a number of different clients. It's a subject close to my heart and, I suspect, to many of you.

For me, they both go right to the heart of not only retail and hospitality but all consumer facing businesses. Not only that but they are a reflection of our society today. They show us not only how demanding we have become but how we are being subtly (and sometimes not so subtly!) educated to expect more from our dealings with brands. They say that the pen is mightier than the sword and that has never been truer than today. That device in our pockets which we never leave home without, sleep with, eat with (and probably a whole lot of other activities which we won't go into here!) is always on, always connected and always ready to allow us to broadcast our feelings, our state of mind, our hopes, our preferences & especially our disappointments.

Those of you who follow me @andrewbusby on twitter might well know where this is heading (!) but allow me to indulge a little further. Working from home for me usually means either grabbing something locally or if there's something in the fridge I'll make myself something. Today I knew I needed to get a replacement ink cartridge for the printer so headed into town. The thing I like about living in East Grinstead is that it has many independent coffee shops and small restaurants, perfect for grabbing a quick bite in the middle of a busy day. So, I planned going to one as it was near where I needed to get the cartridge; great – 20 minutes or so and then back home and on the laptop again.

The toastie Gods were however, conspiring to defeat this honourable objective. Now I don't know about you but I can usually tell as soon as I walk into a coffee shop or restaurant if they're under pressure, not having a good day or just plain hopeless. On this occasion, it was the former however I made the decision to stay with it as I'd been there before and the food and service were usually fine. Speaking recently to a restauranteur friend of mine about service and waiting times, he said the maximum time subconsciously allowed by people before being seen after they have sat down is 8 minutes and a similar time after that waiting for the food once the order has been placed. That's the timescale after which we begin to get twitchy – I'm sure you're familiar with the feeling. We can feel that resentment rising, the emotional response starting to take control. Well, after waiting over 20 minutes for a simple toasted sandwich, that's exactly what happened to me today. When, after 30 minutes it was finally brought to me, I wasn't really in the mood to enjoy it. But this was eclipsed by the fact that they had got the order wrong despite me being very clear when I ordered it. Result? I walked out (after all, I couldn't wait another half an hour for the correct order) vowing not to go back. In that example, the service delivered was woefully below expectations resulting in a terrible experience. Time was when we might have mentioned this in passing to family or friends; today we can share our thoughts with the world with just a few words and the click of the send button.

Now, with emotional response subsided there is a great opportunity for that particular restaurant to turn things around however my suspicion is that they will ignore my sentiment. This is a mistake still made today by many brands even though the opportunity is there to demonstrate turning a detractor into an advocate. If I'm proved wrong, part 2 of this blog will be borne - sadly, I somehow doubt it will see the light of day. And in case you were wondering - yes, I did tweet about my experience.

A Modern Day Arkwright, A Retail Journey Back To The Future

First published in Retail Reflections, 7 April 2018

I thought I knew retail; maybe you thought you did too? Time for a reality check. Truth is, retail isn't just to be found in the retail parks and in the shopping centres or for that matter - online; no, to find retail at its purest you need to venture somewhere a little different. And so, my journey took me to the outskirts of leafy Reigate in Surrey, there to meet with Dave Williams, the extremely affable proprietor of Bettahomes. To call this a hardware store would be to do Dave a disservice for this is hardware meets garden centre meets pet shop meets yarn meets......well, pretty much everything! On the same site for the last 27 years, it is clear that Dave is doing something right, I was intrigued to know the secret to his success.

After the somewhat sterile experience we all have in some of the large chains, spending time with an indie retailer like Dave was like a breath of fresh air. And it only took a few minutes to see why as the first of a string of customers came in whilst I was there. These didn't feel just like customers however - they were more like old friends, all greeted with the same cheery "hello, how are you today". But more than that, most if not all, knew Dave and it became clear that they came to him not just for great prices but because they trust him. "Often all they know is what they're trying to do, not what tool(s) they need to do the job. They come to me for that advice" Dave said.

In a space no larger than your average living room, Dave manages to carry over 4,000 different lines; crammed floor to (literally ceiling) not a square inch of space goes unused. However, the mix has changed over the years. "I used to sell plenty of kettles and toasters for example" he explains, "two or three of each a week; now I'm lucky if I sell one a year since the Tesco Extra down the road expanded. My whole store is less square footage than their toaster and kettle aisle!" In another fascinating insight, he adds; "People under 45 don't fix things anymore, so my stock has changed to reflect this".

I asked him what the most popular lines are: "Bird seed followed by light bulbs and black bags". And as if to underline the point, one of Dave's customers enters the shop in need of a new light bulb for her lamp which she is clutching. It unfolds that she went to the aforementioned superstore but she says they seemed totally baffled so she came to Bettahomes and admits she should have come here first. Not only is the light bulb supplied but also fitted - not a big task but another example of the service Dave's customers have come to expect. But it's when we start discussing his customers' shopping habits that the true picture unfolds.

Located on a small parade of shops, in the 27 years since he's been there, Dave has seen many changes. Where once there were other similar convenience type shops, now he has a kitchen design and a hairdresser for neighbours. "People come here specifically for something, there's no longer any passing trade" he says. And in a somewhat perverse twist, they still sometimes buy the same items at higher prices in the big chains, bemoaning the fact when they see he carries it at a much lower price. And of their monthly spending habits? "Last week of the month, just after payday I see plenty of these" says Dave, holding up a £20 note. As the month goes by however, these begin to disappear in favour of coins. "It's getting earlier and earlier in the month now" he adds, indicating that shoppers' spending is being squeezed more and more.

"I often get customers come in to the shop, check out a higher value item and then they will come back and purchase it once payday comes around". It's a window not only into retailing but the local economy and all the better for it. Perhaps a little scruffy round the edges, for this writer it all added to the wonderful patina which is Bettahomes; like your favourite pair of slippers - good, honest down to earth retailing at its best. And in the final analysis, Bettahomes manages to do something which every retailer aspires to - they really know and look after their customer. If you're ever in the Reigate area I urge you to go and take a look.

Why Retailers Need To Remain Relevant

First published in Forbes, 23 December 2018

This isn't a 'Ten Retail Trends For 2019' piece - that comes later, however, 'remain relevant' might just be the single most important trend to pay attention to for any retail business as we rapidly approach the New Year.

relevant

/ˈrɛləv(ə)nt/

adjective

"Closely connected or appropriate to what is being done or considered". Staying closely connected with your customers is not optional. The choice they have, often at just the touch of a button or a swipe right, is not only extensive but accessible like never before. As consumers, we are promiscuous and unpredictable creatures, like the electorate we can be prone to wild swings as the mood takes us. And often for no apparent reason. We expect, no, demand, brands to constantly be 'in the moment', constantly updating and changing to reflect current tastes. Staying close to your customers outweighs price and product.

And in the digital age in which we live, this is by no means an easy task; social media means that we are forever updating ourselves in real time: who's hot and who's not. One which most definitely falls into the latter is Topshop. For years, the go-to brand for teenagers and twenty-somethings, its sales have been tanking for years. The combination of a lack of investment in its online business and trendier new brands such as Boohoo and PrettyLittleThing, have firmly relegated Topshop to the second division. So, what did they do?

In April 2014, in a desperate bid to win back customers, Topshop announced that ' the icon is back' - Kate Moss, the first supermodel turned designer, who left years earlier, was back. There was only one flaw in the plan: whilst Kate Moss is undoubtedly a very successful supermodel and global icon, to many of Topshop's younger customers she is old enough to be their mother. But not only that, amongst their target demographic, social media is having a greater and greater influence on who they choose to spend their hard-earned cash with, compared to others, hers is a somewhat muted voice. A quick look on Instagram is revealing: whilst Kate Moss has over nine hundred thousand followers, top fashion influencer Alexa Chung has over three times as many. In other words, to a large proportion of Topshop's customers, Kate Moss is no longer relevant.

Topshop, however, is not alone, there are many other brands, especially in fashion, who are having to show a certain stoical sangfroid in the face of determined and unrelenting pressure on sales and margin. Even that darling of keyboard commerce, ASOS, is showing signs that not all is well with the share price crashing nearly 40 percent after a recent profit warning. And this, even though they are not saddled with the cost of running a store estate. Ahead of Christmas, in the final dash to the line, most if not all, are resorting to ever more daring discounting in an attempt to shift stock. The problem is, whilst this may provide a short-term hit and keep the tills ringing, it is unlikely to have any lasting impact. Because in an 'Instagrammable', selfie-strewn world, relevance trumps discounting every time.

The Mary Poppins Of Retail How One Apprentice Star Created A Retail Phenomenon

First published in Forbes, 22 January 2019

Frances Bishop is a mix of incredible energy, unrelenting passion and a healthy line in delightful self-deprecation. And in a relatively short space of time, this former Apprentice finalist has built a burgeoning retail business. I've long felt that it is the young retail entrepreneurs who hold the key to the future of the high street and was keen to find out her secret to success. I wasn't to be disappointed.

Launched five years ago, what began as a single store selling designer childrenswear at outlet prices, has since grown into a £1 million business with three stores and a fourth soon to open. I had arranged to meet Frances and it was as if a force of nature had entered the room, charming and personable and from the get go it was non-stop. The physical incarnation of this energy and enthusiasm are the three Pud stores, located in Doncaster, Mansfield and Newark - all have Frances' DNA running through them. 'I have a social responsibility' she says. And when asked why she started the business, illuminatingly it was 'because after having my son, I found that all the existing children's stores were so stuffy'.

The Pud Store has no online transactional website, indeed if you visit it, you are greeted with the message that it is under construction. Frances is unfazed by this and says that all their near 30% of online business comes via their Facebook group. One gets the feeling that this is no ordinary retail business and so it proves. The mention of traditional retail KPI's are met with a scornful look and a grin which is never far away. Indeed, she has very little time for the more traditional high street chains and scoffs at their heavy top-down command and control structures. Clearly, Frances is in tune with her customers; but this is no mere platitude, she lives and breathes it.

'We will do anything to get our customers back into the store' she says, adding 'we can control the footfall'. This is no immodest claim, The Pud Store boasts a loyal customer base who place their trust in the business and keep returning time and again. As Frances puts it, "We create these pockets of joy".

The way the stores are run is simple, straightforward common sense, but still anathema to many. Store staff - 'her girls', are empowered in ways similar to the model so favoured by that other great business, Timpson. Each store has a 'Franual' by which to run the store but staff are encouraged to use their own initiative and if something doesn't feel right, to exercise their own discretion.

Tearing up the rulebook

How many times do we hear retailers blaming the weather for poor sales? When I mention this, I'm greeted with a look of resigned condemnation. 'We were selling sandals when it was snowing' she says, 'and we sold out'. She has no advertising budget and no branded carrier bags, 'our customers love us for that'. Another sign that this is no ordinary retail business. She encourages her staff to use social media to connect with their customers, something many much larger retail businesses could learn from. And there is no staff uniform, just name badges. When in the store, they wear slippers. 'Because they are comfortable and we want the store to be fun, to be a happy place. Often, we're down on the floor, playing with the children or helping them to try on a new pair of shoes.

She clearly recognises that when Mums come into the store, they could be a little stressed out, and in need of just 'taking a moment' to regroup. 'When that happens, we'll often put the kettle on and help them unwind'. Frances keeps coming back to the thought that none of what she's doing is revolutionary and in a charming way seems genuinely surprised at the attention the business is getting. Many larger chains now beating a path to her door to learn the secret sauce.

But it's not all down to slippers and empowerment, it is clear that Frances is directly involved in the detail of the business, poring over the numbers endlessly. When we met, her phone was pinging continuously, showing the constant stream of transactions processed through The Pud Store Facebook group. Where next? I ask. The business plan allows for growth from three to ten stores in the next 18 months which would mean by 2020 it would be a £3 million business. Who said that bricks and mortar retail was in trouble?

Everything about Frances is straightforward ('what you see is what you get'), no nonsense, common sense. On the evidence of this, I for one don't doubt that The Pud Store will rapidly go from strength to strength. A retail success story to celebrate and on the face of it 'practically perfect'.

The Sweet Smell Of Success

First published in Forbes, 1 February 2019

There are business relationships and then there are business relationships. And then there is the relationship between U.K. retailer The Fragrance Shop and e-commerce provider, OmniCX. If you are a hard-pressed retail CEO, struggling to align everyone behind one common vision, seeking closer, trusted, working relationships with your partners, take heart from this story. It shows just what can be achieved when one visionary retail CEO met an equally like-minded CEO of a young, digital e-commerce business.

Established in 1994 and now with over 200 stores across the country, The Fragrance Shop is firmly established as the largest independent, U.K. fragrance retailer. Its CEO, Sanjay Vadera, has worked tirelessly to bring the business to the enviable position it enjoys today, always with a laser focus on the customer. While others may profess to put the customer first, listening to Sanjay discussing his business philosophy, it is clear that he lives and breathes the customer. Innovation and a constant quest to convey the brand in the best possible way characterize his thinking. This is borne out by the recent eight-week trial of something called the 'Sniffbar' - stand-alone pop-up fragrance bars located in high traffic density locations such as Birmingham New Street station.

The success of them, '80% of customers who used them were new to The Fragrance Shop', according to Sanjay, means that more are planned to be rolled out after the initial trial. Fragrance shopping is a sensory experience, and he's connecting the physical with the digital. He's on a journey, a journey which is continually evolving to bring not just relevancy and personalized experiences for his customers but to make all the connections that matter so much when customer expectations are themselves, rapidly evolving.

According to Sanjay, he simply wasn't able to find the desired e-commerce functionality straight out of the box. A partner was needed who not only understood this but was able to translate this into an e-commerce solution which would realize Sanjay's vision of putting the customer experience right at the heart of everything the business did, regardless of the touchpoint with the customer. The success of the relationship has resulted in what some may describe as a slightly unusual step but one which Sanjay sees as entirely good business sense - inviting OmniCX to join the board of The Fragrance Shop.

Sanjay sees this as a logical step to take, "we are on a journey and this way, OmniCX experiencing the pain points from within the business will benefit both parties". For Vikram too, it means not only being able to experience first-hand but also to input to the discussions being held at board level within his customer. Unusual or not, it reflects a deep and trusting relationship rarely found and one which many would no doubt be envious of. Retail businesses like to forge close working relationships with their (often) multitude of technology partners but rarely has there been a relationship quite like this one.

How Did I Do?

First published in Forbes 6 February 2019

Based on my last Forbes article, how likely are you to recommend me to a friend on a scale of zero to ten? Sounds familiar? They can be found everywhere; they even appear when we're asleep, they ambush us when we're least expecting them and they drive us crazy. You know what I'm talking about, customer satisfaction surveys of course. They have become part and parcel of almost every consumer (and more besides) interaction we ever have. But are they really effective?

The last time I flew to the U.S. earlier last month, I received a survey via email from the airline asking how the flight had been and that was before I'd even landed! My personal favourite, however, is of one at the exit of the public toilets at Victoria Station in London with the caption 'did our facilities meet your expectations?'. Yes, they did thank you, I expected them to be gross and they were. Which goes to show that the question being asked and the context in which it is being asked matter. A lot. Car manufacturers have embraced customer surveys with a vengeance. When collecting my car from having its annual service recently, I was asked to complete a survey and gave them an overall eight out of ten, which I thought was pretty good. 'Oh sir', came the response, 'why have you marked us so low?' It transpired that anything other than a ten would result in the dealer being taken to task by the manufacturer.

This to me would appear to be a fairly pointless exercise, obfuscating any real underlying issues. Seeking feedback in this fashion to satisfy some opaque corporate metrics seems to be the very opposite of customer centricity. On the other hand, when was the last time you saw an airline boasting of having a 99.9% success rate?

Customer sentiment in-store

All this is giving rise to a new retail metric, perhaps the most critical one of all, namely, how is my customer feeling? The days of running a retail business on sales per square foot alone are rapidly receding. Savvy retailers are now realizing that understanding customer sentiment drives something far greater than just short-term sales figures. To help understand this, I spoke to Georgina Nelson, Founder and CEO of feedback company TruRating.

'Traditionally, there has been something of a disconnect between customer experience and store operations' she says, adding 'how do you operationalize customer experience in the store?' Eschewing the traditional means of capturing customer sentiment that most review sites provide, capturing customer sentiment in real time at the point of purchase has proven to be very revealing for online purchases and in-store alike, but it is in identifying gaps in the latter experience where much of the interest lies. 'It's not just about spend in the moment, it's about the customer's propensity to come back and spend more', Georgina adds. And with an astonishing 85% response rate, it is proving to be a pretty accurate barometer of store performance linked to the customer experience.

Georgina gives the example of one customer, London based Chinese restaurant chain Ping Pong, who now have had more ratings than Disneyworld! Intriguingly, just asking one simple (anonymised) question at the point of transaction is providing insights which have their roots in psychology more than anything else. Just addressing the customer by name, for example, has shown a 30% increase in average transaction value.

In the relentlessly competitive and challenging landscape in which retailers now find themselves, capturing customer sentiment might just be the difference between survival and oblivion. Maybe I'll ask the question again, how did I do?

Love Them Or Loathe The, Serial Returners Could Just Be Your Best Customers

First published in Forbes 2 July 2019

The school prom is only days away and you still haven't got that killer outfit. No problem, just logon to your favourite online fashion site and order up a bunch of stuff; on the basis that at least one will hit the spot. Fast forward to the morning after. What a great night! The black number did the job and it's now time to return it along with the dozen other outfits you ordered. After all, it's not a problem, you get free shipping and returns so why not take advantage of it?

That scenario is being played out in homes up and down the country with increasing frequency. Make no mistake, returns are big business. And it would be easy to view it as an epidemic, a disease killing eCommerce and eroding margins. In the U.S. alone, Statista estimates that return deliveries will cost $550 billion by 2020, 75.2% more than four years prior. Worse, that number doesn't include restocking expenses nor inventory losses. And with ASOS recently announcing that it was increasing its returns deadline from 28 to 45 days, it is clear that the industry is bowing under consumer pressure.

The Amazon effect – seamless, easy convenience combined with continually raising customer expectations – is being felt right across the industry. And for good reason. A study published in the *Journal of Marketing* showed that retailers that offer free returns see customers spend up to 457% more than they did before initiating a free returns policy. The converse was true, too. Repeat purchase spending dropped by 75%–100% for customers who were asked to pay for return shipping. But is all this sustainable? And in this context, "sustainable" meaning from both a commercial business perspective and from the impact on the environment. Consumerism running out of control? One could easily believe this is the case.

It conjures up an image of climate change protestors vying for space with increasing numbers of white vans navigating our towns and cities, delivering and collecting those all-important parcels.

Returns Equals Great Customer Service

But if all this strikes a decidedly depressing note, there is hope. Having a customer friendly returns policy is of course, a necessity in today's ultra-competitive retail landscape. The trick though is to have a smart returns policy. And that doesn't necessarily mean penalizing serial returners. I wanted to get a view from an organization whose very reason for being is to handle our insatiable appetite for online shopping. Mike Richmond, chief commercial officer at Doddle had this to say:

"Returns are not a new challenge for retailers. Never before have we had as many conversations with retailers about how they make their returns proposition more profitable—or less unprofitable."

It is possible to implement processes and procedures to reduce the volume of returns without alienating the customer. However, it does take the entire organization operating as one, to one set of rules. And the key to unlocking this seemingly intangible is: data.

"Retailers have to tread the finest of lines between a convenient proposition that drives customer satisfaction and loyalty, whilst simultaneously tackling the challenge of high-returning products or customer segments. To do that properly, retailers need the right returns infrastructure to give them accurate and actionable data, and many just aren't set up that way," says Richmond.

Today, retailers are drowning in data. But historically they have not known how best to use it to most effect. According to Newmine using artificial intelligence to provide a thorough and constant analysis of customer data, transaction data, product sourcing and customer sourced feedback data can reduce and optimize returns rates. And there are examples of brands using returns as a driver for growth and profits by focusing on it to deliver great customer service. Zappos now offer a 365-day, free two-way shipping and return policy. Yes, you read that correctly – a whole year. Quite something when one considers that the implication of this is that inventory could be out of the business for nearly a year.

"Our best customers," says Zappos' VP of services and operations, Craig Adkins, "have the highest return rates, but they are also the ones that spend the most money with us and are our most profitable customers." Counter-intuitive? Well, perhaps so, but it goes to demonstrate that as consumers we not only expect but recognize what we perceive as great customer service and reward it with our loyalty.

What Barbados Can Teach Sainsbury's And UK Supermarkets

First published in Forbes 19 July 2019

I happen to live in East Grinstead, a mid-sized West Sussex market town; you may know it. And if you do, you'll know that it's an eclectic place. Filled with a wonderful mix of Turks, Poles, scientologists, buddhists, tree huggers and people who send their children to schools that teach them how to hug trees. You name it, East Grinstead is a broad church. I'm told that it's the ley line that runs right up the centre of the high street which accounts for much of this variety.

Personally, I love the diversity, and as we know, diversity is a good thing. But there's one thing that East Grinstead lacks, and that's a decent supermarket. Well, if you discount the excellent Waitrose, but that's really just for those who don't need to bother themselves with life's irritations, like knowing the price of a loaf of bread. No, for the majority of people living in the real world, East Grinstead is a veritable oasis when it comes to doing the weekly shop. Which is surprising when you come to think of it. What it does have however is a branch of Sainsbury's. And in common with many other Sainsbury's, this is to supermarkets what Hannibal Lecter is to veganism. You get the picture.

I meant to put this to Sainsbury's boss Mike Coupe, when we had lunch not so long ago but tales of Brexit stockpiling and the (then) impending marriage with Asda, rather got in the way. Which is a pity because I could have described the awfulness of experiencing one of his stores on a weekly basis. Because, as you may know, under his stewardship, Sainsbury's have embarked on a programme which can only be described as being designed to explore the outer extremities of customer experience. It appears to be working, the latest figures showing that sales are down 1.6%. Need avocados? Only on a Tuesday between 10am and midday. Berries? No chance unless it's a full moon. And as for finding your favourite brand of yoghurt? Don't even try.

Wonky Bananas

All this rather came to mind earlier this week when I was enjoying a break in Barbados, that Caribbean island paradise, famous for rum punch, Sir Gary Sobers and Rihanna. As always, the weather was amazing, but that wasn't the only thing. I needed to venture to the local supermarket for one or two essentials I hadn't packed and it was there that it suddenly became only too clear why Mr Coupe's next holiday really ought to be in Barbados.

You see, Barbados' Massy Stores have managed to create supermarket heaven. Granted, much of the fresh produce hadn't exactly become weary by their arduous journey, and the fish had probably just taken a bigger leap than usual to land in the fishmonger's sea of ice, but more than that, this was a spectacularly presented store. Wherever one looked, there was something I'd grown unaccustomed to witnessing: fully stocked shelves. In fact, the availability was incredible, especially when one considers the location. If Barbados ever did Brexit, the only stockpiling would most likely be on the mango trees which abound. And not only that, for I could take my basket with less than ten items and visit a (manned) checkout which was especially designed to serve other like-minded souls. For one grown accustomed to having to either queue behind someone with a trolley wilting under the strain of another oversized load or having to work the checkout myself, this was something of a luxury.

Launched in 2014 in Barbados, Massy Stores are located throughout the Caribbean. So, if you're ever in Barbados, or St. Lucia, or St. Vincent or Trinidad and Tobago for that matter, and need to stock up on one or two essentials, it just might be worth you paying a visit. Just don't expect to pick them up in East Grinstead before you go. Seems a hurricane has swept through West Sussex and all the essentials have been blown west. Which is why my next weekly shop may take a little longer than usual.

PART FOUR: IT'S A BUSINESS ISSUE

The traditional top down, hierarchical, command and control business model is rapidly being proven to no longer be fit for purpose. The trouble is; many of the old, traditional retailers are either unwilling or unable to change. Stuck in the past, in a siloed organisational structure, adhering to out of date (and often conflicting) KPI's, like the dinosaurs, they don't realise that they are a dinosaur and are consequently rapidly losing their relevance. Without which they have a very limited lifespan.

To succeed in the demanding world of the consumer customer experience is everything – but we've all heard that many times before, right? A great view of the state of the nation in internet retailing and technology was on offer at a recent Internet Retailer Conference & Exhibition in Chicago – a gathering of retailers, vendors, analysts, which I attended as an IBM futurist. The lens we looked through was that of the consumer. Brands no longer own their own brand. The consumer does. Content and context are king. Engagement and experience are the foundations upon which all else is built. Retail is experiencing a seminal moment and those who realise and recognise this will be the ones who survive. So, what resonated in Chicago and what made it memorable?

Fun

It's important to have fun and have a sense of fun. Be fun to deal with and ensure that this is what your brand stands for. Have fun internally and this will permeate through to your customers. For a sense of fun, Spanish children's retailer Imaginarium is a great example. Their stores don't have doors, they have archways – one large size for the adults and a much smaller one for the children. It's all about creating a sense of fun and wonder for the children.

Engage

Consumers want and expect special brand engagement more than ever before. After all, they own your brand and have a strong influence over it so why wouldn't you want to engage with them on multiple levels? Forrester Research asked retail execs what their number one investment priority for 2017 was. The answer was personalisation. According to Olapic, 76% of consumers view content posted by other consumers as more honest than advertising. And in the world of fashion, Instagram, with over 700 million monthly active users, is the most popular means of engaging.

Big names such as Harrods and Burberry use it extensively to bring the catwalk right into their customers' lives.

Personalise

Recent Forrester Research asked retail execs what their number one investment priority for 2017 was. The answer was personalisation. That one-to-one relationship with the consumer is still a little way off. Being able to join up all the dots and be able to pick up the 'digital trail' that we all leave behind us every day will be the key to being able to effectively personalise your offer. It follows that people seek to be inspired by their retail experiences, which is good news for stores. But with over a million different home pages for different customer types, Shop Direct is doing a pretty good job. Personalisation will rapidly mature from the current, retrospective 'ambulance chasing' into a highly sophisticated contextual method of engaging with consumers and driving conversion.

Inspire

The industry has long talked of 'retail theatre' and indeed there are consumer-facing businesses who actively promote the concept in-store of the shop floor being front of house – the stage, where the store colleagues are the actors. Restaurant and pub chain Hall & Woodhouse goes beyond that and even has a staff green room in each restaurant. Creating an emotional attachment and excitement around a brand is therefore central and key for retailers. So, it follows that people seek to be inspired by their retail experiences, which is good news for stores because only there can shoppers feel and touch in ways that they can never do online. The two now, of course, coexist, finally putting an end to the concept of omnichannel. Except that too many retail businesses continue to cling to the notion that we shop in channels. Time will teach them that this approach is fundamentally flawed.

Excite

Retail is different to almost every other industry in that consumers have an emotional connection with retail brands in a way which doesn't exist in relationships with, say, utility companies, telcos or public services. Creating an emotional attachment and excitement around a brand is therefore central and key for retailers. New York-based mattress company Casper is fast developing a cult following and excites and inspires in equal measure whilst Shoes of Prey could well be laying down the template for how people buy our shoes in the future.

Artificial intelligence

I've left this to last because it is, I believe, what is required in order to fully deliver all the above. That might sound like a bold statement. However, artificial intelligence and machine learning technologies are set to transform retail in ways that could not have been imagined until recently. The phrase 'know your customer' is about to take on a whole new meaning once cognitive and machine learning become part of every operation across a retail business. Artificial intelligence represents the most profound change in retail in over 100 years and the journey is just beginning. 1-800 Flowers in the US or North Face are two great examples where artificial intelligence technology is driving brand engagement. And the journey is just beginning. A journey which will not only transform retail but also consumers' lives. Personalisation will become true one-to-one relationships where needs and wants are anticipated and goods delivered where and when people want them.

Why Brands Fail

First published in Retail Reflections 3 August 2017

Last week American Eagle announced that after only three years it was pulling out of the UK market. Add to that the names of those who have exited or are struggling - J.Crew, American Apparel, Forever 21, Hollister and Banana Republic immediately come to mind - and you begin to see a trend appearing. What's behind this? Why are these brands failing? On the face of it, all should be performing well. Good stores, good locations and in most cases good customer experience. However, look a little closer and a different picture emerges.

Take American Eagle; three stores one in each of Westfield Stratford and Westfield Shepherds Bush and one in Bluewater. Those sites don't come cheap. Add to that the market they are in; attracting 15 to 25 year olds with an affordable 'preppy' look – an age group notoriously fickle when it comes to fashion preferences. Oh, and add in the small matter of fast fashion icons such as H&M and Zara and it makes for a strong headwind. Put all that in the context of a decidedly challenging UK retail fashion landscape where, faced with rising costs and a slowdown in consumer spending, most of the more well-established brands are struggling. You get the picture.

But for me there's another, perhaps more vital ingredient which is lacking. More than ever, brands are having to compete like crazy to get into our consciousness. According to research firm PMR, "the recall of one brand blocks off the other brands from the range of alternatives in which the consumer makes his/her selection". So, it's already extremely difficult to achieve any kind of brand awareness. But when one considers the penetration and influence which social media has today, the task of gaining brand recognition in a new market assumes almost herculean proportions. In a recent blog from Brandwatch, up to "96% of conversations happen outside the official, owned channels of the brand". Therefore, it follows that the brand no longer owns the brand, the consumer does. More than ever before, we need to understand what a brand stands for, why it is in business and what value it can offer us.

It's an intriguing proposition; does brand loyalty still exist? The effects of austerity continue to be felt and perhaps our shopping habits have changed forever. A brand must understand its why before anything else - why it is in business and must be able to articulate that why in an effective manner. Unfortunately, too many continue to simply broadcast their message. In today's socially aware, savvy consumer, brands also need to engage with their audience. It is about inspiring consumers; in his excellent book 'Start With Why', Simon Sinek states "we are drawn to organisations that are good at communicating what they believe". More than ever before, we need to understand what a brand stands for, why it is in business and what value it can offer us. In the case of American Eagle this message was lost, with fatal consequences.

One Bad Apple?

First published in Retail Reflections 29 December 2017

"Our customers' trust means everything to us. We will never stop working to earn and maintain it". So proclaimed Apple in December 2017.

The following scenario is fictitious, any resemblance or reference to persons present or past is entirely coincidental.

The corridors of the Cupertino headquarters reverberated to the sound of gnashing teeth; sales of the new iPhone were not going according to plan. Q4 sales figures did not make for great reading; the January earnings call was going to be 'prickly'.
"We've got to do something" barked Tim, "And fast". Gathering his team, a plan was swiftly hatched.
"We'll ship a new iOS, one which will slow down older models. That way the poor schmucks will soon want to upgrade"
"You think it will work?"
"Piece of cake - we'll schedule it overnight in all time zones and label it a security upgrade - they'll never suspect".
Of course, whilst there is no suggestion that the above conversation ever took place, it was widely reported this week that Apple have admitted to deliberately slowing down some older iPhones in order 'to preserve battery life'. Rather than the technical (we could, I imagine, debate that ad infinitum) this raises questions about the trust we as consumers place in a brands' integrity. This example calls out Apple - arguably possessing the most brand appeal of all - others such as banks, retailers and airlines have, in the past, all also fallen foul of the same problem. It begs the question as to what kind of corporate culture exists in an organisation prepared to treat its customers in such a fashion? And, should we as consumers accept being treated in this manner?
Perhaps the reasons for Apple taking this action were legitimate however it was the manner in which they were implemented which is of most concern; doing so without the knowledge or control of customers. There was no opt out capability. At the time of writing there are multiple lawsuits in the US from users seeking action as a result of Apple deliberately slowing the performance of their iPhones. This amounts to a massive breach of trust on the part of Apple, the only smartphone manufacturer which controls every aspect of their device - hardware and software. However, such is the brand following (I hesitate to call it loyalty but Apple gets closest) which Apple has built up over many years, it is highly unlikely that Apple fans will desert them for Android on masse. But consider this for a moment...... Apple CEO Tim Cook has called

autonomy "the mother of all AI projects". During an August 2017 earnings call, Cook re-emphasized Apple's deep interest in the technology.

Given the customer experience Apple has delivered to its iPhone customers, the prospect of Apple autonomous vehicles brings with it a nightmare scenario too easy to imagine. But perhaps as consumers we get what we deserve?

When the first iPhone was released 10 years ago no-one questioned the battery life or whether it was right to spend so much on a device which was, in reality, completely controlled by its maker. As Christof said in The Truman Show: "We accept the reality of the world with which we're presented". And perhaps that is above all why Apple will weather this particular storm and why in 10 years' time, it won't only be the streets of Cupertino which are filled with Apple self-drive technology.

Bungled Bunnings - A Case For Review

First published in Retail Reflections 5 February 2018

The news today that Wesfarmers, owners of Bunnings, is to close up to 1 in 6 of its 240 Homebase store estate comes as no surprise. Announcing an A$1bn write down of the business, Wesfarmers MD, Rob Scott admitted that 'a lot of the issues we are dealing with today are self-induced'. Whilst the honesty might be refreshing, it is the reasons given for the shambolic state of affairs which are, frankly, incredulous. A management team with little or no knowledge of the UK market led to the dropping of popular product lines combined with underestimating the winter demand for others, such as heaters (this is the UK not Bondi Beach after all).

Two years ago, just prior to the sale of Homebase from Home Retail Group to Wesfarmers, it was trading profitably albeit not spectacularly so. And let's not forget that then HRG CEO John Walden announced a store closure programme of up to 25% of the estate under the Homebase Productivity Programme. However, the appointment of new CEO Echo Lu from Tesco in March 2015 was bearing fruit with like for like sales hitting 5%. Clearly there was a more customer centric approach to the business and this was having a positive impact.

But, just weeks after completion of the sale of the business in February 2016, the entire Homebase Board had been ousted. Quite possibly the most blatant case of corporate arrogance in recent memory. In a statement this week, Michael Schneider, head of the Bunnings group, said: "A significant amount of change has been driven through Homebase since the acquisition and the disruption caused by the rapid repositioning of the business has contributed to greater than expected losses across the Homebase network". The news that Bunnings UK Managing Director Peter Davis is retiring alludes to where Wesfarmers feel the blame lies. But this is to deflect from the real issue.

Misunderstanding both the market and the customer for a business successful in their home market is nothing new - think Best Buy, Tesco Fresh & Easy for starters. But throw into the mix a breath-taking arrogance and you have a recipe for disaster. Homebase employs 12,000 people, many of which are now facing an uncertain future - the store closures won't be announced until June (yes, you read that correctly) and this perhaps is the most disturbing aspect of this sorry tale. Not taking the basic trouble to understand your market and your customer is amateurish at best; putting people's livelihoods at risk through corporate arrogance is unforgivable.

Five Things We Learnt At Retail Week Live

First published in Retail Reflections 15 March 2018

That retail extravaganza, otherwise known as Retail Week Live, once again took place at the Intercontinental O2 in London last week. From the main Flagship stage to the Pop-Up to the Launchpad where young start-ups got to showcase their offerings, the only frustration was that there was so much content, it was impossible to get around to cover it all! So what were the five stand-out topics which we picked out from two solid days of retail immersion?

Artificial intelligence

If you're getting a little jaded by all the references to artificial intelligence - don't. It wouldn't be an understatement to say that AI is the future of retail. And for those who don't yet have it as part of their strategy; act now else be left behind. Chatbots and voice are only the tip of an ever-growing AI iceberg where the potential is almost limitless. Sky CEO Jeremy Darroch referred to it as the "biggest game-changer" whilst Ocado CTO Paul Clarke claimed that they would not have a business without it. However, there are still those who are yet to appreciate not only the immense potential of AI but of the absolute necessity to embrace it as part of their strategy. Chatbots and voice are only the tip of an ever-growing AI iceberg where the potential is almost limitless. Those brands who don't will doubtless not be around in the near future.

A new dawn?

A sense of deja vu may have prevailed when Government Minister for Retail, Andrew Griffiths spoke about a new alliance with retail (remember Portas and Grimsey Reviews - stakeholder apathy killed both). But with the announcement of the creation of a new Retail Sector Council chaired by Richard Pennycook, a sense of optimism prevailed. Griffiths said: "It's time for the retail sector and the Government to work together to understand the issues, and come up with solutions to tackle productivity, the skills shortage and the challenges of new technology."

Spaced out

No, it wasn't the alcoholic gummies on offer, but the topic of stores and in particular, better ways to create wonderful spaces for people to enjoy.
Whilst there are notable exceptions to the rule (think ASOS, Boohoo etc) in the main, it is understood that stores have been, are and always will be a vital part of any retailer's armoury. It's just that they now need to be so much better than before. In the week when Toys R Us finally succumbed to the inevitable - largely owing to the sorry look of their store estate - the retail industry can learn lessons from other closely related cousins. In an excellent session, Dishoom Founder, Shamil Thakrar discussed the amazing story which is Dishoom; modelling their restaurants on the Irani cafes of 1950's Bombay. Shamil asserted that "discovery & transportation are more important than prominence" and aping the Backyard Cinema philosophy he added that "stories allow you to layer things".

And in a separate session, Trevor Hardy, CEO of The Future Laboratory talked about creating 'sanctuary spaces' where people can go to unwind, relax - free from the stresses and strains of modern living. Maybe the future of retail is all about how we manage and create inspiring spaces? Retail would do well to take note.

Data: the new currency

With GDPR just around the corner, it felt appropriate that data and the critical importance of being able to not only manage it but analyse it, interpret it and then act upon it fell into sharp relief at the conference. In a keynote interview with Retail Week Editor in Chief, George MacDonald, M&S CEO Steve Rowe admitted that M&S is "drowning" in data and that "we can't join it together". He wasn't alone; but help is at hand if retailers care to seek it out.

Throw away the rulebook

"Sales per square foot is not a key indicator for us....if we started from scratch tomorrow we wouldn't build a business like most retailers are today". So said Lee Woodard, Global Chief Experience Officer at Crabtree & Evelyn. And his views echoed many at the conference. What worked for decades just doesn't any longer and this is proving to be a tough pill to swallow for many. The retail KPI comfort blanket is slowly being stripped away and this is proving to be an uncomfortable journey; one which won't be for all, but for those retailers who survive, a vital and inevitable one. Discarding not only those traditional KPI's but the entire organisational structure which supports them in favour of something entirely new is a fundamental challenge which must be overcome.

Weather: Are You Getting It?

First published in Retail Reflections 2 October 2018

Saturday October 21st 2017; if you're a Huddersfield Town fan you'll know the significance of this date. But as the chances are that you are not, allow me to explain. Huddersfield were at home to Manchester Utd in the English Premier League. Coming off the back of a thrashing at Tottenham and Utd on a roll after conceding only twice in their previous 8 league games, no-one gave Huddersfield much of a chance. They however, had other ideas. At the end of a pulsating (not to say very wet) afternoon, Huddersfield emerged winners 2-1. Luck? A poor Utd performance? Elements of both were in evidence but it was one of the post-match comments from Utd manager Jose Mourinho which perhaps sheds the most light on the contrasting performances: "They had the better attitude, more desire".

A clue can be found in looking back at the weather in Huddersfield that day. It was a rainy old afternoon in Huddersfield! Because on Saturday 21st October 2017, Storm Brian was battering England with winds over 70 mph and heavy rain. Indeed, all day Saturday a yellow weather warning was in place for northern England. Could Huddersfield manager David Wagner have prepared his players far better than Mourinho did with his for the storm they were about to face?

Working with weather

OK so we can't control the weather, right? And this writer for one hopes that we never reach a time when we can; the thought is just too terrible to contemplate. So, if we can't control the weather what can we do about it? It seems that with virtually every poor sales announcement comes a weather warning these days. It was too cold, too hot, too warm, too wet - we've heard them all. But does it really have to be like this? Of course not. According to Jim Dale, Founder & Senior Meteorological Consultant at British Weather Services, "If it's not number one, then weather will be pretty near the top of influencing factors on when and why customers purchase what they purchase". The reality is that for most retail businesses, the weather is regarded as an external factor which cannot be predicted and therefore doesn't appear to be included in any business planning. If the weather plays such an important role in retail sales performance why then doesn't it feature more prominently when planning and forecasting?

It comes down to a question of attitude; rather than 'being done to' by the weather, surely the time has come to work with the weather to gain competitive advantage? Retail Week has recognised 'weather' as being a retail influencer, ranking it at number 58 in the 2018 'Power List'.

But judging by the number of retailers who blame the weather for poor sales perhaps it should be much higher? We shop for comfort and out of necessity, with weather being the main driver. If retailers do not educate themselves on the impact on retail sales, they are missing out. Accurate forecast is one thing but weather education and its place in a retail organisation are both in need of wholesale review. It touches every part of the organisation from marketing to supply chain from merchandising to store operations. And now with artificial intelligence available to all, there really is no excuse to blame the weather for poor sales.

Complex algorithms constantly updated in real time - something no human could possibly do - means inventory can be in the right place at the right time according to whatever the eternally fickle British weather might be doing. Isn't it time we began working with the weather rather than accepting it as a consequence of doing business?

The Famous Five - How To Survive Today's Retail Storm

First published in Forbes 26 October 2018

Welcome to my first ever blog as a Forbes contributor and it coincides with yet more bleak news from the retail sector. Because it was this week that one of the UK's most iconic department store chains announced its annual results. We thought it might be ugly and so it turned out; so if you are of a nervous disposition, look away now. Record pre-tax loss of £495m (including an £80m write-down of now redundant IT systems), like for likes down 2.3%, dividend suspended and - wait for it - 50 stores (equivalent to a 3rd of the estate) to shutter over the next 3-5 years. Yes, we knew that Debenhams was finding life in 2018 retail tough but perhaps not quite this tough. However, CEO Sergio Boucher tried to remain upbeat: "It has been a tough year for retail in 2018 and our performance reflects that. We are taking decisive steps to strengthen Debenhams in a market that remains volatile and challenging".

Stripped of much of his turnaround budget, it wouldn't be unreasonable to imagine more than a backward glance at Amazon, his previous berth. For a business founded in 1813, the harsh reality of today's cutthroat retail environment is biting and biting hard. Disappointingly that turnaround strategy now appears to be founded on cost-cutting and placing almost the entire house on beauty. I don't know about you but I've never seen a retail business cost-cut their way out of a crisis. And all this coming as Debenhams prepares to enter what must now be considered a make or break peak trading season.

Be famous for something

Before we look at the 'Famous Five', let's first look at why it's important to be famous. By nature, department stores are big boxes which consume huge amounts of CapEx in order just to stay still let alone be constantly refreshed and updated - something which is expected by today's demanding consumer. But it can be done; just taking a look at the likes of Harrods, Selfridges, John Lewis to name a few, shows that the model can be made to work. But they are in a different place and space; they have a clear idea of self and relentlessly push this. The old adage is never truer when applied to department stores: be at one end or the other but never get caught in the centre of your chosen market - this is the toughest place to be. Be famous for something, not for nothing.

Our shopping habits are evolving at a speed never before dreamt of and our expectations are now increasing at an exponential rate; leaving many retail brands behind. The wake we are creating is becoming greater and greater and it is these rough waters which are steadily sinking many a struggling brand. So, what is the answer? To reverse years of underinvestment is not the work of a moment; but for those able to, here are five things which should be on any must do list - 'The Famous Five' if you will.

Understand your brand

In other words, what does your brand stand for? Why are you in business? What are your brand values? Those that you would be willing to die for in order to protect. If you and everyone in the business are not able to answer these as if they were second nature how on earth do you expect your customers to understand you and therefore want to buy from you?

Put the customer first

Everyone does this don't they? Well, perhaps it's time for a reality check and to ask yourself if you actually practice this. What is it really like to put the customer first? When was the last time you walked - yes, literally walked - your customers' journey? From the moment they are within 500 meters of your store to when they are inside it. Focus on those elements you are able and unable to control. Because you need to understand how your customer is feeling, what mood they are in when they enter your store.

Let change be a way of life

It never ceases to amaze me how many retailers are fearful of introducing change to their store network for fear of.......what exactly? As we've seen, your customer's expectations are growing rapidly, don't be left behind.

Act like an indie

One of the most liberating things in retail is to go and talk to an independent retailer about how they run their business. Not having the shackles and command and control mentality which burdens most chains, they act on their instincts, they know their customers, they are part of the local community. When it is more important than ever to deliver authenticity, empower store staff to run their store as if it were their own business; not as a satellite chained to a faceless head office function.

Treat store associates as your greatest asset

Long seen as the biggest cost (after property) store associates are in reality a retailer's biggest asset. They are your brand ambassadors; liberate them with the right tools and attitude and overnight you can gain many thousands of new salespeople. No-one ever said it was easy and now is just about the most difficult and challenging time to be in retail. Always remember: people need a reason to engage, to visit - be famous for something and your customers will love you for it.

Why Your Most Important Asset Is Out There Now Representing Your Brand

First published in Forbes 26 November 2018

You're a retail business; what's your biggest cost? I bet most would answer 'property' closely followed by 'my people'. Yes, it's a sad reality that most retailers still consider their staff to be one of their biggest costs. Retail can learn a lot from other consumer-facing sectors, hospitality being one. There is a hotel in the U.K. called The Chewton Glen. Situated in the heart of the New Forest, it is regularly voted the best in the U.K. and in the top 100 in the world. The building is marvellous, the Spa luxurious and the restaurant, a historic fine dining gastronomic delight. And yet, none of these vital elements makes it the special hotel which it is. No, the difference is the people.

For this is non-intrusive pampering at its very best. From the moment you arrive to the moment you depart, you are made to feel special. The memory of the experience living long in the memory.

Retail theatre returns

There was a time not so long ago when all we seemed to be talking of was 'retail theatre' - how to deliver a great customer experience - and then the term rather went out of fashion; to be replaced by the somewhat ungainly 'experiential' retail. Well, breaking news - retail theatre is back, and with a vengeance. Because if stores are to continue to even exist let alone thrive, not only does the very fabric of them need to excite and inspire but more importantly, the people who staff them. They might not be actors but they might as well be. They are the beating heart of your stores but all too often they fall victim to what Bob Phibbs, aka The Retail Doctor describes in his blog as 'retail hypnosis'. They're not bored, it's just that they lack stimulus. They have a vital role to play, one which is far too often under-estimated; for it is they and they alone who represent your brand. Their day should be such that they aren't interested in checking their smartphones every few minutes because there's so much else to get excited about.

Think like an indie

It is always an illuminating experience whenever I talk to an independent retailer. Why? Because they have a completely different and liberating outlook to that of a chain.

Whereas a typical chain operates in a rigidly hierarchical, top-down command and control manner, an independent has total freedom to decide what is best for their customers. They decide their pricing, they decide their visual merchandising, they decide their social media presence, they decide their……well, just about everything come to mention it. At this point, I can almost hear the cries of derision! What? Leave them to it? Where's the corporate governance in that? (said the disgruntled CFO). Where's the adherence to planograms? (cried the incredulous merchandiser). Where's the consistency of our messaging? (remarked the mortified marketeer).

Far from advocating an anarchic culture, there is a truth in that retail store operations staff are under-utilized when it comes to creating great customer experiences. For too long seen as a costly overhead, it is ironic that their roles will become far more highly valued with the increasing growth of online traffic. Because if stores are to remain, they don't need to be just good, they need to be great. And this means that the service we receive from humans (as opposed to robots, indeed any form of automation) needs to be great too. And the good news? Automation and those robots will remove much of the drudgery of working in a store, freeing up the people to handle the more interesting tasks. Like interacting with customers.

New skills will be required and needless to say a different approach to attracting and recruiting the right people will be needed for those who embrace this new retail world. We are all humans and fundamentally, shopping in store is a human experience which needs to be many things but above all, it should be enjoyable. In the race to deliver better and better in-store customer experience, perhaps it is time to consider your greatest asset and your greatest opportunity; your people.

From The Dalai Lama To Hostage Negotiation: A Meeting With Jacqueline de Rojas

First published in Forbes 5 March 2019

'Where the channels......where they convene, in the future, will not necessarily be a place'

Jacqueline de Rojas

Jacqueline de Rojas CBE glides imperiously across the room to greet me, effortless charm personified. But as becomes apparent, this is combined with a razor-sharp intellect and clarity of thought; no wonder she is in demand to sit on boards up and down the country. Jacqueline is nothing if not busy - President of techUK, President of Digital Leaders, Co-chair at the Institute of Coding, a non-executive director of AO, Rightmove, and Costain. She also serves on the government's Digital Economy Council and has previously been voted the Most Influential Woman in IT. She was awarded CBE for Services to International Trade in Technology in the Queen's New Year Honours list 2018.

She is passionate about diversity and inclusion and it was this, in the context of her work with retailers, that I was fascinated to find out more about. We begin with her work with the board of Home Retail Group, this at a time when it comprised Homebase and Argos (how times change). And as a lesson to all businesses, she describes how as a board they asked themselves 'what business are we really in?' This is not as straightforward to answer as one might imagine as Jacqueline recalls the tale of a U.S. carwash owner (who went on to make many millions) who opened a carwash business believing that his customer was every car owner in the country and that he was simply providing a carwash service. Only once he had realized that his customer was much closer to home and that by adding additional services, what he was actually offering was not just a car cleaning service but a status business, that things really began to take off. The lesson being: learn what business you are in and never deviate. Diversity and inclusion are never far from the surface of our discussion - for good reason, Jacqueline talks of 'diversity in the design and the algorithm' while explaining that in the early days of the car seat belt for example, women and children died because seat belts were designed by men.

She recalls her meeting with the Dalai Lama and of being a little apprehensive at the prospect but it seems that many retail boardrooms could use her calming and wise influence at the moment. And in that context, Jacqueline describes the 'intensive' ten-day hostage negotiation course that she recently attended which was, in reality, a course in teaching 'non-violent communication'. Meaning that how the words are spoken is far more important than just the words themselves. And, as she says, if you're speaking to someone with a gun in their hand, you tend to adopt a more conciliatory tone than you might otherwise.

From her time on the boards of Home Retail Group and AO.com, amongst others, she is in a very good position to observe what we as humans want: "First and foremost we want to be heard, closely followed by the need to be included". And her role as a non-executive director? "Identify the shortest route to success, which isn't necessarily a straight line". We discuss the role of a retail business these days and whether the sole purpose is to deliver shareholder value, something which I venture must be occupying the minds of many retail chief executives just now. "I believe we can balance profit with purpose", she says. And how does that translate to the AO.com business, one which is famous for the empowerment its front-line staff are afforded? "Do what would make your granny happy", comes the reply.

Personalization and the use of personal data in retail are both topics currently being keenly debated and I wonder what Jacqueline's views are. It's about seeking a balance between convenience and privacy; "can we afford to be off the grid anymore?" she asks, adding that "we want convenience but we don't want to be spied on". And of course, much of that is a very personal thing which varies from one individual to another, "our level of tolerance is tied to our level of experience", Jacqueline adds. We conclude on the future of retail and what we are likely to see in the next 12 to 18 months. Jacqueline's answer is revealing: "Where the channels......where they convene, in the future, will not necessarily be a place".

Personally, I have never had the privilege of meeting the Dalai Lama, but after spending time with Jacqueline de Rojas, I feel I've come close.

As Kingfisher Parts Company With Its CEO The Question Is, What Does Plan B Look Like?

First published in Forbes 20 March 2019

With sales and share price subdued, it appears Kingfisher has finally lost patience with its CEO Véronique Laury and her turnaround strategy, announcing today that they would be parting company. But are they in danger of throwing the CEO out with the bathwater? The news comes amid a worsening crisis at the group which once counted Woolworths, Comet, and Superdrug amongst its brands, together with DIY names, B&Q, Screwfix and Castorama. Profits in the last twelve months have slid 13% despite a 10% rise in sales at Screwfix.

Laury joined in December 2014 and set about transforming the sleeping giant with a turnaround strategy for the group, dubbed "One Kingfisher" - set to cost £800m over five years in return for £500 in annual savings. The plan relies on unifying product ranges across brands, boosting e-commerce, and seeking efficiency savings. However, three years into the strategy, sales continued to flag - this at a time when B&Q should have been cleaning up in the U.K. market, its principal competition, Homebase, being driven to the wall in the hands of new owners, Wesfarmers. Whilst Homebase continues its fightback under the ownership of Hilco, Kingfisher shares have fallen 27% over the last year. But can all this be laid at the door of Laury?

I recall my time at Kingfisher in the early 2000s, and that global sourcing was an issue then: batteries sold at Comet, Woolworths and Superdrug were all sourced separately at different prices. So, one has to question what has been going on to drive efficiency savings these past fifteen years? And of course, the DIY market has not only been hit of late by the downturn in consumer confidence caused by Brexit uncertainty, but it has also been caught out by a change in behaviour by one of its key cohorts of customers: millennials. And that's because millennials don't do DIY, they prefer 'do it for me'. From car light bulbs to flatpack furniture requiring no screws or tools, this new attitude to maintenance is a growing trend and the traditional DIY sales to the public, as opposed to the trade, is suffering.

Knowing your way around Instagram and the intricacies of your average smartphone don't seem to translate into knowing how to put a shelf up or change a light bulb. All this has spelled bad news for Kingfisher, the effectiveness of the turnaround being masked by underlying weaknesses in the fundamental business performance. While investor patience has practically evaporated, and as one of the last surviving female FTSE 100 CEO's prepares to depart, the real question is: does Kingfisher have a plan B?

The Reverse Ferret And The Department Store: How Today Became Debs Day

First published in Forbes 29 March 2019

Bored of Brexit? Weary of Westminster? Tired of Theresa? Jaded by Jacob? I could go on, however, I imagine the answer is yes to all of the above. And as if to add to the comedy routine, this morning in the Commons we heard Labour MP Mary Creagh branding the Prime Minister's attempt to win MPs' approval today to her withdrawal agreement, a 'reverse ferret', claiming the bid to split the proposal into two separate votes broke previous promises to the House. For those bemused by all this, the term reverse ferret originates from Kelvin MacKenzie's time at The Sun and is a phrase used to describe a sudden reversal in an organization's editorial or political line on a certain issue. Why do I mention all this? Because if the shenanigans being played out in Westminster right now were not enough, there's another soap opera, with parallel similarities, taking place just down the road in the - soon to be ex-offices - of Debenhams at Regent's Place.

The fortunes of Debenhams these past twelve months or so have been well documented, however, this week they reached their climax - or denouement - whichever way one chooses to look at it. Yesterday, we heard that Debenhams bondholders had backed Debenhams' restructuring plans, in a snub to Mike Ashley's Sports Direct, which is trying to buy the business in return for Ashley running Debenhams. Sports Direct, as we know, had previously offered £40 million to prop up the ailing Debenhams business and after this was rejected, Ashley (a majority shareholder with nearly 30% of the shares) managed to oust Chairman Sir Ian Cheshire and remove CEO Sergio Boucher from the Board. Yesterday's offer was increased to £61.4m, on condition that Ashley becomes chief executive and Debenhams drops its refinancing plans.

Fast forward just a few hours to this morning and the picture looks a little different (are you sensing the Brexit parallels now? Keep reading, it gets better)
With Ashley calling for Debenhams' advisors to be 'put in prison', speaking this morning, Debenhams Chairman, Terry Duddy announced: "We are pleased to have agreed this comprehensive funding package which secures the future of the Debenhams business, we have also preserved a route for our shareholders to participate in the future of the business, but this requires the support of our major shareholder."

While the deal will make £101 million available for Debenhams to draw down, the remaining £99 million is subject to a - you guessed it - backstop, with even the dates, closely aligned with Brexit. For the additional £99 million to be available, by April 8th Sports Direct, or another major shareholder with more than a quarter of the company's shares, must make a firm offer for the retailer, including refinancing

Debenhams debt, the department store said. Alternatively, Sports Direct could drop its attempt to oust all but one of the Debenhams board, and either agree to underwrite a rights issue or provide funding on terms agreed by Debenhams' lenders. In the event that neither of these happens, the company said that the remaining funds would be made available only when the company's lenders take over the business, but added this "would very likely result in no equity value for the company's current shareholders". Shares in Debenhams jumped more than 40% on the news of the refinancing deal being completed.

Just what Mike Ashley's next move will be is open to conjecture but of one thing we can be sure, just like Brexit, no-one really has a clue. Did anyone mention a reverse ferret?

Bonmarché: Is Private Equity The Real Reason For The Death Of The High Street?

First published in Forbes 2 April 2019

Edinburgh Woollen Mill, Austin Reed, Jaeger, Jane Norman, Peacocks and now Bonmarché, textile tycoon Philip Day has added another struggling brand to his rather enigmatic stable of fashion labels by capturing a controlling interest in long-suffering high street women's retailer, Bonmarché. Piqued no doubt at losing out to Mike Ashley in the race to capture the ailing House of Fraser, he has suppressed his ire for this moment, offering shareholders just 11.5 pence per share, a 36% discount on Monday's closing price. This after agreeing a deal with former private equity owners Sun European Partners to acquire a 52.4% stake in the business.

This values it at just £5.7 million, a fraction of the value when it was floated in 2013. And of course, there is a certain irony in Bonmarché being acquired by Philip Day, who also owns Peacocks. In 2002, Bonmarché was acquired by Peacocks Group, only to sell it to Sun European Partners in 2012 for an undisclosed sum. What goes around comes around. But while Sun European Partners pocket £40 million from selling their share of the business, what of the staff who work there? It is here that this becomes an all too familiar narrative of store closures and consequent job losses. Is it any wonder that retail struggles to attract new talent? By the very nature of it, retail, more than ever, needs to be allowed to take a long-term view. This is why, even in these troubled times, no-one is especially concerned by the relatively poor results posted by the likes of John Lewis, their partner model ensuring that they are able to play the long game.

Bonmarché aside, this approach is not so of private equity of course. Their motivations are far removed from the long -erm viability of the retail businesses they invest in. And of course, in today's volatile climate, they could reasonably argue that were it not for their investment, many retail names would have fallen into administration long ago. But when have you ever witnessed private equity investing in the very fabric, the infrastructure of a retail business? Stories of staff having to do running repairs themselves are rife and, in many cases the aging buildings are, in some cases, literally falling down. This, of course, is of no concern when you're extracting maximum value and putting little in.

Business rates, online competition, and rising costs may dominate the headlines but it's in the nature of the ownership of many well-known high street brands where perhaps the most concern should lie. Laden with debt and with little investment - no wonder many are unable to compete with the newer, leaner more agile online businesses who are rapidly dominating the market. Bonmarché may not be the most fashionable of retail businesses, it probably doesn't have any millennial or Generation Z customers but that would be to miss the point. Choice is a precious commodity and variety should be embraced. Just as we strive ever harder for diversity in the workplace, so we should do likewise when it comes to the high street, for the alternative surely leads us inexorably towards a desperate and dystopian future.

Why The CMA Were Wrong And Where Now For Sainsbury's And Asda?

First published in Forbes 26 April 2019

The news that the Competition and Markets Authority (CMA) had blocked the proposed merger between Sainsbury's and Asda, was not entirely unexpected but what are the implications for both businesses and for us as consumers? What did the CMA say and what were the reasons they gave for rejecting what would have created the U.K.'s largest supermarket chain, accounting for £1 in every £3 that we spend on grocery shopping? Sainsbury's has more than 1,400 shops in the UK, of which about 800 are convenience stores, while Asda has more than 600.

Earlier this year, Sainsbury's and Asda promised to sell between 125 and 150 of their supermarkets to allow the merger to proceed, along with some petrol stations and convenience stores. Quite some concession. But this wasn't enough to persuade the CMA who said that the merger would lessen competition at both a national and local level. Stuart McIntosh, chair of the CMA's inquiry group, told the BBC's Today programme: "It would reduce competition in supermarkets and online grocery shopping and at the companies' petrol stations. "We think that it is likely to lead to higher prices or other changes which would be unwelcome to shoppers, such as longer queues."

Either the CMA hasn't heard of the likes of Tesco, Co-op, Aldi, Lidl, Iceland, Morrisons, Waitrose and so on or they must know something we don't. Longer checkout queues? Higher prices? In the ultra-competitive world of U.K. grocery retailing, why would Sainsbury's and Asda put up prices? And as for longer queues..... The CMA also claimed that it would be difficult to monitor the pledge to reduce prices. Er, Stuart - ever heard of mySupermarket.co.uk? George MacDonald, Executive Editor of Retail Week had this to say: "Their proposed merger was not an appeal for a helping hand but could have kept up the pace of competition to the benefit of shoppers through, for instance, efficiencies and lower prices. The CMA was surely wrong to kibosh the deal".

How many people in retail would really agree with this conclusion from the CMA – that a tie-up would likely lead to "price rises, reductions in the quality and range of products available, or a poorer overall shopping experience?" The CMA has demonstrated a lack of understanding of the grocery market and the broader retail landscape in the U.K. and by blocking the merger they have done a massive disservice to the British consumer.

What of Sainsbury's and Asda?

While the consumer has lost out, they are not the only one. The differing reactions from both Sainsbury's and Asda yesterday revealed much about their relative positions. Asda boss Roger Burnley said he was disappointed: "We were right to explore the potential merger with Sainsbury's, which would have delivered great benefits for customers and supported the long term, sustainable success of our business". Asda owner Walmart wants out so they now need to find a buyer, this could be to a private equity investor or stock market listing. Largely, though, it remains business as usual.

George MacDonald: "The fact that Asda and Sainsbury's were willing to consider linking up, resulting in a big three, is stark evidence that the market is not monolithic. They aimed not to leg over the consumer, but to compete better on the shopper's behalf". The story over at Sainsbury's however, is rather different, one can almost sense the gnashing of teeth in the corridors of their Holborn headquarters. Boss Mike 'we're in the money' Coupe, who had personally championed the deal since its announcement 12 months ago is in a rather different position than his counterpart over at Asda, saying that the regulator was "effectively taking £1bn out of customers' pockets".

This was his big play and he pretty much staked the house on it. To see it fail so spectacularly will mean that some serious questions will be asked. And he doesn't have long to find the answers, with Sainsbury's annual results being released next Wednesday 1st May. After selling the merger with Asda to the market as being key to the success of the business, he will quickly have to come up with a credible plan B. If he doesn't, the chances of him surviving look slim indeed. With store standards being lambasted from all sides, Sainsbury's suddenly looks like a business which is showing signs of creaking. If the top supermarkets were likened to Premier League clubs, Sainsbury's are now struggling for a place in Europe next season. It seems more than a little ironic that the regulator, who is mandated fundamentally to protect the interests of the consumer, has instead dealt a blow from which it could take years to recover.

Landlords Braced To Be Hit By The Retail Transformation

First published in Forbes 21 May 2019

If you are of a certain age, you will remember the retail landscape Croydon was once famous for. Iconic department stores such as Kennards, Grants and Allders. Then there was the Surrey Street market, all vibrancy and colourful characters. And then, of course, there was the Whitgift Centre. Named after the local John Whitgift school and opened in stages between 1968 and 1970 it has been a Croydon landmark for decades. It remained the largest covered shopping centre in Greater London until the opening of Westfield in White City in October 2008. More recently, and with the opening of Westfield, it had begun to look a little long in the tooth and so the news in 2013 that Westfield and Hammerson were planning to re-develop the site into a mega-mall, was greeted by the good people of Croydon with understandable optimism. Fast forward to May 2019 and the picture looks less rosy.

With the current uncertain outlook, building is yet to commence and the scheme is 'under review'. Originally planned to open in 2021, this has dealt a devastating blow to the borough. We're all too familiar with seeing empty units on our high streets and in our shopping malls, but perhaps the retail property crisis behind this is the unseen creeping death. And for landlords, the situation is rapidly escalating into a full-blown crisis. Rental income is declining as struggling retailers either fall into administration or use insolvency measures, usually in the form of company voluntary arrangements (CVAs) in order to lower their rent burden. It's a vicious circle and shows no sign of letting up. Meanwhile, we expect better and better and no longer tolerate mediocre. On the day of writing, Jamie Oliver announced that his chain of "Jamie's Italian" chain had gone into administration. The continued march of the new and, let's face it, more exciting and vibrant high street is relentless. According to *The Times*, four of Britain's largest listed property companies could have £6 billion in total wiped off the values of their portfolios over only three years because of pressures on the retail sector.

The crisis impacting retail is now shining a light on property values. According to the IPD index, from the beginning of 2018 to the third quarter, property values in the retail sector fell just 2.6%. Analysts were predicting falls of 20% in the wake of administrations and CVAs. Valuations remaining unrealistically high is akin to a ticking time bomb. Property valuations are based on factors such as recent sales of similar properties, market conditions, and future rental income. Having a disproportionate relationship between claimed values (from landlords) and the reality means that an implosion of the market is almost inevitable.

The Croydon Partnership, which is responsible through Westfield and Hammerson, for the plans to redevelop the Whitgift Centre, maintains that the delay is temporary and until 2023. As more and more retail businesses vacate the crumbling

Whitgift Centre, however, it is leading to a vicious spiral of rapidly dwindling footfall from which it may struggle to ever recover from. And in that scenario, with property values plummeting, will the people of Croydon ever get their much-anticipated mega-mall?

Why The Demise Of Arcadia Is Bad News For All Of Us

First published in Forbes 28 May 2019

The long-anticipated announcement of a Company Voluntary Arrangement (CVA) at Arcadia has now materialized, well actually, seven CVAs—one for each of the brands. Of one thing you can be sure, Sir Philip Green does nothing by halves. And whilst the original announcement listed 23 store closures across the brands—including the jewels in the crown, Topshop and Topman, reports now suggest that this number has more than doubled, and now includes the flagship Miss Selfridge store on Oxford Street. Added to that, the great American dream is over for SPG. Oh, and the small matter of dropping out of *The Sunday Times* rich list. How the mighty are fallen. Let's all join in and give him a right royal kicking, shall we?

After all, he's not exactly the most lovable character on the high street, and if recent allegations concerning his office behaviour are to be believed, he's still firmly stuck in the '90s—at best. And therein lies the problem for Arcadia—just like its owner, it's still stuck in the '90s. And while the pretty new things are shining brightly (perm any from Boohoo, Missguided, ASOS, etc.) Topshop has resolutely stood still. The investment decisions that were needed 15 years ago simply didn't happen, in favour of extracting yet more and more value from the company. What's that you say, darling? A £1.2 billion dividend? Oooh, thank you! Well, when was the last time you tried using a debit card to fill up your superyacht? You get the picture. So yes, it would be all too easy to jump on the bandwagon and join in the chorus of from the side-lines, after all, in this cutthroat world, he jolly well deserves what's coming to him, right?

Retail: it's a very human thing

But as always in life, there's another side to this story. One which is very human and touches all of us. For the loyal 18,000 people who work at Arcadia and in their stores up and down the country, the current crisis affecting the business is all too real. And whilst we're on the subject, spare a thought for those greedy landlords. The decade's old gravy train is hitting the buffers and hitting them hard. Because they are the ones who will bear the brunt of the impact of any CVA in terms of reduced rents. Philip Green's main task right now is to persuade them that the alternative to a CVA and consequential reduced rents is insolvency. Something they may find hard to swallow given the lavish lifestyle he leads.

And what of us? The consumer? Should we shed a tear at the demise of a once powerful retail brand? Well, yes as it happens. Because this is also being enacted up and down the high street (think Debenhams, House of Fraser and in the last few days Monsoon Accessorise). And while we may dislike the wealth of these retail entrepreneurs, the fact remains that they provide employment for many tens of thousands of people, and us with affordable fashion in a way that we've never previously enjoyed. Yes, we can carp on about how they are all dinosaurs and never moved with the times but the fact remains that they are now in an unfair fight. One which is completely weighted against them ever being successful again. Of what am I referring? Business rates of course. If ever there was something in need of urgent reform it is that. It's something I have written about before and will continue to do so because it is the single biggest threat to our high streets and therefore our communities, that we've ever faced.

With a level playing field in place for *all* retail businesses, we may still see the likes of Monsoon, Topshop, Debenhams, etc. continue to struggle but at least they will be able to compete on equal terms. And then, and only then, will we really be able to gauge the impact and relative success of online businesses, because in the end it's all just shopping, right?

PART FIVE: THE PATIENT NEEDS MORE THAN LIFE SUPPORT

In part four, I made reference to business rates and that is a recurring theme in this book. And for good reason for it is the single biggest threat to retail, and specifically, physical retail. As we know, many column inches are pre-occupied with the 'retail apocalypse' and 'the death of the high street'. Both of which we know to be a fallacy, but only if 'the patient' is given the right treatment. Retail plays a central role in all our lives and communities and as a sector without better support, there will be socio-economic consequences for all our communities. Sadly, this point appears lost on those who are in a position of being able to influence the course of the evolution of the high street.

It is however, a truth, that the high street has relied on retail for far too long. In the '80s and '90s, the large chains set about cloning every high street up and down the country, opening more and more stores – the measure of a successful growth strategy back then. This resulted in high streets which were, in the main, fully populated but were indistinguishable, one from the other, and, crucially, resulted in retailers ending up with far too many stores. Remember that it wasn't until 1995 that Amazon was born. Life was very different back then.

Today, we see the consequence of those years of growth, at a time before anyone envisaged the impact which the internet and online shopping would have. Why is all this important? In every town up and down the country, the high street forms the centre of the community. And the high street, still to this day, largely relies upon retail to provide it with its pulse. That of course, is changing. But twenty years ago, just how many coffee shops would you expect to find? We are talking about an era before Starbucks, before Costa, before Subway. If we roll back the years a little further, we are talking about an era before McDonald's – in the U.K. at least. Life was very different back then.

Of course, times change and nothing stands still forever. Today, we have a far more diverse and interesting mix of businesses to enjoy when we visit our town centres. But by and large, those same high streets still rely on retail. Which means that they are relying on a sector which is going through a massive transformation, the likes of which most of us have never experienced in our lifetimes. This means that the challenges facing retail are not a retail problem per se. They are a socio-economic problem, one which requires all the stakeholders to collectively work together in order to navigate these troubled waters. Sadly, to date, there is precious little evidence that this is happening to any great effect.

But that should not prevent us from remaining optimistic, besides, retail is by far the most interesting, exciting and downright rewarding sector to work in.

However, one of the things that always surprises me is that it doesn't do a better job of promoting itself as a viable career option. Unfortunately, the majority of school-leavers and graduates, view retail as simply a fill in job to earn a little money whilst they search for a 'proper' job. But with retail they've already found one. It can be so much more than working on the shop floor although this is where most if not all begin their retail journeys. The industry body, the British Retail Consortium does a good job of trying to change these misconceptions about retail but it requires the industry to also help itself. And this, at a time when technology is changing the very nature of what it means to work in retail. Those very same school-leavers have the innate digital skills which retail businesses are now crying out for. They are digital natives and this has huge implications. They already have the right mind-set and aptitude for many of the roles which are now appearing in retail that simply didn't exist even five years ago.

Working with data, robotics, autonomous vehicles, artificial intelligence, social media, digital marketing, digital content creation – all these and more are now available in what has become one of, if not the most innovative of industries. It has had to, faced with the twin forces of the ultra-competitive environment and escalating consumer expectation. Retail might be a human first industry but it is technology which is driving it. More than ever, retailers need to adopt the mindset of a young technology start-up if they are to compete and survive.

But they cannot do this alone, just with business rates, it will need all the stakeholders to work together in order to attract and retain the necessary skills which the industry so badly requires. The apprenticeship levy has simply added yet more cost for retailers and hasn't delivered on its promises. Again, just like business rates, the apprenticeship levy needs to be reformed but done within the context of promoting retail as a great career option. Not simply to get more people into work for the sake of the figures.

As someone who has a daughter who has worked her way up from a Saturday job in the local store of a well-known high street fashion retailer to a senior head office role within the same business, I have witnessed first-hand the hard work and sacrifices she's had to make. Working six days a week, 5.30am starts, working Bank Holidays, Christmas for her for as long as I can remember has been a day to rest and recover before it all starts again on Boxing Day. But I've also seen the satisfaction and sense of fulfilment derived from working in such a demanding and intensive environment. It sometimes needs a little processing when you think that a twenty something in charge of a large store is in effect running their own multi-million pound business. This is often overlooked but this is why many do choose to forge a career in retail. Long may it continue.

Black Friday Blues

First published in Retail Reflections 27 November 2017

'Twas the Friday after Thanksgiving and all around one could hear the sound of clicks and tills. For this wasn't just any Friday – this was BLACK FRIDAY - that annual pilgrimage for bargain hunters everywhere. I travelled to Oxford Street to see first-hand how it was shaping up this year – and with a scare at Oxford Circus, I nearly got more than I'd bargained for!

More marmite than marmite, you either love Black Friday or loathe it, for me - I just get those Black Friday Blues:

"Went down to the shops, see what I could find -grab me a bargain, that's what I had in mind. Nothing but crowds and 20% off, all I got me were those Black Friday Blues"

OK so it might not be on the way to becoming a hit but you get the general idea. For me, Black Friday no longer represents bargains, it's a day when we all go a little bit bonkers. Clearly, it's matured since that crazy day in 2014 when people were trampled in the rush to grab a 42" widescreen TV (you can pick up a nice LED model for just £250 now) however, it still remains a magnet for both retailers and consumers alike. But aren't we all just kidding ourselves here? Does Black Friday actually grow sales or simply move them forward into November?

And for consumers, quite apart from the question of whether they are really picking up a bargain, isn't it simply a case of timing? Surely better to save the money from November payday and watch as the bargains keep coming in the run up to 'The Big Day'? Some, such as Dixons Carphone, swear by it; CEO Sebastian James declaring his love for it on Twitter. But others are not so ebullient. The list of those who prefer not to take part is growing.

Harrods – "We believe it cheapens the brand"

Fat Face – "It's bad for customers, bad for business and bad for UK retail" CEO Anthony Thompson

Jigsaw – "Black Friday warps our perception of what's valuable and important" CEO Peter Ruis

Black Friday is fast becoming a paradox. According to a PwC Consumer Survey conducted in November 2017, nearly half of consumers said that they would either actively avoid it or were simply not interested. But an early look at the figures from PCA Predict shows that after a sluggish start during the morning, down on last year, it picked up during the afternoon to overtake 2016. And of course, the event has now stretched to nearly a week making comparisons difficult to make but one thing's for sure, whilst it might polarise opinion, as long as there are retailers desperate to grab market share and bargain hungry consumers – Black Friday won't be going away anytime soon. But I'll leave the last word to Primark who, on their website neatly sum it up thus: "Black Friday? *Yawn* As if we'd make you wait all year for a flash sale, just to wow you with our totes increds (sic) prices. Savvy honeys know where to shop for them low, low prices - regardless of what day it is". Amen to that.

NRF 2018 - A Look Ahead

First published in Retail Reflections 7 January 2018

Only days away, Retail's BIG Show - National Retail Federation (NRF) in New York is nearly upon us. Retail Reflections will be in the Big Apple to cover it, so what do we expect to see at this year's Show?

Artificial intelligence: the next chapter

Artificial Intelligence (AI) is already taking hold in many different ways however we believe that it will be a common thread throughout most retail initiatives in 2018.
The desire to be able to personalise on a one to one basis at scale dictates that AI must be a part of a retailers strategy and those who have yet to embrace it are already behind the curve. Whether it be our smartphones, Alexa, Google searches, predictive data analytics, social media......the list is almost endless, AI will pervade like never before. Until now it has sat on the periphery for many organisations, we expect it to move centre stage at NRF.

The store is dead, long live the store

"Reports of my death are greatly exaggerated" - so said Mark Twain, and the same can be said for stores. Of course, they were never threatened; in reality what we've been seeing is a natural culling as the retail model shifts and big malls and out of town retail parks become unfashionable. So, whilst we expect to see a continued reduction in space, those stores which are left will be better than ever before. Stores will be where the really cool, imaginative and compelling customer experience takes place. Which is why we are excited to see what developments in store design will be on show at NRF. We've come a long way since all this meant was throwing a few digital screens at a store, today stores have a much broader brief than simply providing a roof to keep the product from getting wet.

Customer experience on steroids

Experiential retail will take on new forms in 2018 and with it, retail will begin to find a new place in our lives. The old model of filling shelves with great product and delighting the customer simply won't be sufficient; indeed, most of the old thinking will have to be discarded as new generations come to demand much more from a retailer. Today stores have a much broader brief than simply providing a roof to keep the product from getting wet. Emotion and feelings will play a much greater part in what constitutes great customer experience. And each new positive experience will reset the bar ever higher as consumers become more and more demanding and less and less tolerant. Those who cling to the old ways will wither and die.

Final mile delivery defines the brand

2018 will see an ever increasing on-demand economy; the context here being that consumers' expectations of delivery capability. The ability to order something whenever, wherever and have it delivered within the hour will become the norm meaning retailers will have to have complete visibility of their inventory in order to meet this expectation. Something few enjoy today.

Rise of the bots

An Amazon and Google infinite loop conversation - perhaps the best definition of insanity there's ever been. We expect chatbots and in particular voice recognition to gradually become ubiquitous during 2018, the writing's clearly on the wall for keyboard interfaces. The smartphone, where a voice interface has been in use for some time now, will accelerate mCommerce through a much easier, more frictionless interface, especially for distressed or convenience shopping. Got used to having Alexa or Google Home around? You get the picture.

So, there we have it, our predictions for NRF 2018 and the year beyond; if you have any thoughts or additional ideas for what we're likely to see this year we'd love to hear from you. Look out for our tweets and blogs from NRF - it's going to be an exciting few days!

NRF Day One: Retail Rallying Cry

First published in Retail Reflections 14 January 2018

If you believe the headlines, Mark Twain may have written retail's epitaph: "The reports of my death are greatly exaggerated" On the evidence of the first day at NRF's BIG Show in New York, instead, he wrote the rallying cry with even Doug McMillon, Walmart CEO quoting Twain during a keynote session in the afternoon. It's not so much a resurgence of retail but a re-branding if you will. They say there's nothing new under the sun and to a large extent that's true but on the evidence of today, what changes is the perspective.

For example, last year, we were hearing about Artificial Intelligence; this year we are hearing about Artificial Intelligence blended with different technologies to create real meaningful value for the customer. That's a fundamental shift. Each day at NRF we are calling out our top two trends which we feel are going to make an impact in 2018.

Blend of technologies

That evidence of the blending of technologies to create a new solution which now adds real value to the customer. AI and facial recognition for example. Before it was one or the other, each in isolation a blunt, incongruous tool. Marry them together and suddenly a proper usable, valuable offering which the consumer can relate to.

Virtual reality

With the convergence of physical with virtual as brilliantly demonstrated by Roots in an inspirational Innovation Lab session, Virtual Reality has finally found a natural home. It felt as if we were searching in the dark for a suitable use case for VR but now Roots have demonstrated that it is possible to create wonderful immersive, interactive experiences by blending the two. Expect more of this in 2018. And mention of the Innovation Lab brings us to a fascinating insight into where both NRF and retail thinking is heading.

Not even standing room at the Innovation Lab

In 2017 the Innovation Lab stage occupied a small area which was never really that busy.

In the two sessions we attended today on AI and emerging technologies it wasn't even 'standing room only' - there wasn't any standing room!

Retail and technology converging even further

Great first day where the heavyweights of Levi and Walmart were out in force so it seems fitting to leave the last to Walmart CEO Doug McMillon commenting on the current state of retail: "If you're bored right now, you're not paying attention".

NRF Day 2: Meet The Future Of Retail

First published in Retail Reflections 16 January 2018

We met the future of retail today - well sort of.....Many would have us believe that the future of retail is here.....now. But that's not quite true. What does seem to be true is that we can at least, possibly for the first time, begin to see what the future of retail might look like. Whilst there may be many pretenders to the throne and the messaging this year (in certain instances) bore a disappointingly familiar look and feel, it is undeniable that NRF 2018 marks the turning of a corner
"We can at least, possibly for the first time, begin to see what the future of retail might look like". So, what did we learn on day 2 of Retail's BIG Show?

Apple taking a bite out of the Big Apple

Need to check on your latest version of iOS and can't wait for 9am the following morning? No matter, Apple have you covered. Their store on 5th Avenue is open 24x7. So, if the urge strikes at 3am in the morning, just wander down to Apple if you need a quick fix. Or if you're a shirt (and whiskey) lover why not pop down to UNTUCKit where you'll be greeted with a wee dram no matter what time of day. Top two trends from day 2?

Services & experiences

It's clear that spending on services & experiences - rather than goods - will continue to grow. And with that, so too experiential retail. Which is all great news for stores. Talking to numerous people at the Show, one thing is agreed upon; there will be less stores in future and closures will continue during 2018 despite the optimistic economic outlook in the US (not so the UK which has it's own rather special challenge!). But the good news is that those stores which remain will be better than ever before and it was interesting to hear the positive take on automation which it is envisaged will free up store associates in particular to do more interesting tasks. Tired of manually checking inventory? Help is at hand!

Frictionless becomes a reality

We've been hearing about 'frictionless' commerce and 'seamless' shopping experiences for years and in truth they've largely been marketing taglines.
Now, finally, the concept is becoming a reality. And interestingly, much of the focus was again around the store as opposed to online. Whether it be easier, speedier checkout or clearer inventory availability our store experience is set to become a much slicker operation than today, predominantly through the empowerment of the store associate. And this is an area where many of the smaller start-ups appear to be thriving.
Whether it be Tulip Retail with their store associate mobile assisted selling and clienteling or Newstore which provides a mobile app to allow easy, quick access to product, inventory, pricing so that the store associate can build a relationship with the customer easily and quickly - one thing is for sure, retail must adopt a different perspective on its frontline store workforce. For too long store associates have been perceived as the most costly line on the balance sheet, instead of the most valuable asset a retail business possesses.
    That outdated, old fashioned way of thinking must change and change quickly; otherwise the naysayers claiming the 'retail apocalypse' is upon us, might just well be right.

NRF Day 3: Saving The Best Till Last

First published in Retail Reflections 17 January 2018

Day 3 was - perhaps fittingly - book-ended by the one technology which everyone was talking about at NRF 2018: Artificial Intelligence. IBM and Watson starred once again at NRF. Why? There seemed to be a realisation this year, not evident in 2017, that in order to survive in the brutal retail environment in which every retailer now finds themselves, AI is not just a technology, it is a lifeline. "We believe in AI" Tommy Hilfiger.

And all the past messages of 'augmented' reality, 'real' reality and so forth finally found fertile ground at NRF. There was a palpable sense that whereas before, AI was perceived as part opportunity part threat, now it is seen purely as opportunity. Able to support human effort and interaction rather than usurping it. In an engaging session in the morning we heard from Salesforce and their take on AI; and whilst our new Dutch (stand up) friend pointed out that 3,250 words have 'AI' in them, perhaps 'Retail' is the most important and relevant word for this discussion.

During an analyst briefing we heard from NRF and IBM on the state of the nation. The challenge is twofold: to understand the non-traditional competition & pick the right mix of technologies to invest in. This has never been truer. And that neatly sums up the challenge for retailers today; just where do I invest my (extremely) limited funds? For young start-ups the question is a simple one; but for the more established, traditional retailers it poses all kinds of difficult questions - many of which are currently unanswered. And from IBM some interesting insights from their research of 15,000 Gen Z from around the world, complete with this somewhat startling fact: "98% of Gen Z prefer to shop in store"

So, with that as the context, what were the top 2 trends which caught our attention on day 3 of NRF? Probably the two most talked about at the Show: Artificial Intelligence closely followed by Stores. But we'll look at the stores first.

The pivotal role of the store

There's nothing more important for a retailer than the store - it's pivotal to success. Pureplay days are numbered. The first might be generally accepted now and this shone through at the Conference but the second? Are pureplay online only retailers really becoming extinct? Well as always, yes and no. The point being, stores are vital. Stores are rapidly becoming pivotal, being at the junction between customer experience, supply chain, digital and physical. They embody the brand and thus it that everything about the store must ooze brand appeal.

Artificial intelligence equals retail

They say that you should leave the best till last and that's exactly what we've done.
NRF 2018 will come to be looked upon as a watershed moment in the history of retail; the moment when Artificial Intelligence came of age, the moment in history when people realised the awe-inspiring potential of this technology. The narrative has shifted - artificial intelligence will provide the platform upon which retail can grow & thrive.

Compared to 2017, we didn't hear anyone discussing AI in itself; the fundamental change was that NRF 2018 saw the narrative shift - now AI was being discussed as an inclusive element of a retailers' brand armoury. We'll be providing some more Retail Reflections on NRF 2018, but for now, Watson - take a bow.

Are We Killing The High Street?

First published in Retail Reflections 10 August 2018

The plight of House of Fraser highlights a worrying trend which has huge implications for us all. The news this morning that House of Fraser has collapsed into administration should be a worry for all of us. And the news that Mike Ashley has snapped it up for £90m shouldn't ease our collective conscience. Whilst it would be easy to point the finger at online, it is a truth that much of the once great department store's woes were self-inflicted.

Along with Toys R Us, Maplin and Poundworld, the business had fundamental problems which it ultimately was unable to resolve. However, there's a wider issue here. And it's a social one. Who doesn't like shopping online? Easy, quick, convenient – everything that a shopping experience should be, right? Well, maybe only partially. In the frenzied dash to embrace everything online, are we in danger of losing our sense of being? Are we risking that very thing that should be at the heart of every town up and down the country? Are we losing our sense of community?

Isolated at our laptops and on our smartphones, our once thriving High Streets are rapidly morphing before our very eyes. And we are all complicit in the change which is occurring. Retail has long been relied upon to sustain our High Streets and it is the High Street which is the beating heart of every community up and down the country. They are the places where we go to not only shop but to meet people, to socialise, to gather to dine, to relax. As humans we are naturally social beings and we need that interaction, that engagement, that stimulus.

But what we are witnessing is a sustained dissolution of our High Streets which begs the question; what is the end game? Assuming that our collective behaviour shows no sign of abating, our insatiable thirst for online nowhere near quenched, what will the town centres of tomorrow look like? Are we, in the quest for better and better bargains online, unwittingly creating a dystopian vision of our future society? The time to act is now. More than ever, we are concerned for the legacy we will leave behind when it comes to climate change and global warming.

Should we equally be concerned for the communities we will leave behind? The plight of House of Fraser as it begins a new chapter in its 169-year history should be a wake-up call for all of us; sadly, the evidence suggests that on the contrary, this will rapidly become yesterday's news. Until the next time.

Business Rates: The Curse Of The High Street

First published in Retail Reflections 12 October 2018

"Business rates are outmoded and outdated. They were created in the last century and are not fit for purpose in the 21st century. The tax burden has reached the point where companies are going bust. Has the Government thought through what happens when retail starts to decline and if the job losses start to become significant"
Helen Dickinson, OBE Chief Executive British Retail Consortium

The news that Coast has collapsed into administration was met with the usual gnashing of teeth. And whilst stablemate Karen Millen has bought the brand and the online business, all Coast stores are shuttered. Brexit, the weather, suppressed consumer confidence, rising staff costs.....we've become used to the usual mantra. But add to this a disease which is attacking our High Streets for which a cure needs to be found quickly lest we witness many more joining the likes of Coast, Maplin and Poundworld. It's the curse of the High Street: business rates.

Put simply, business rates are a tax on property used for business purposes, calculated based on a property's 'rateable value'. The rateable value being a property's estimated value on the open market. The Local Government Finance Act of 1988 introduced the current system of business rates in 1990, five years before either Amazon or eBay were launched and six years before Tesco offered its first online shopping. Retail currently contributes £8bn to the Treasury through business rates - most of it from High Street businesses as opposed to pureplay online retailers. In other words, the current system of taxation on retail businesses did not envisage ecommerce and is therefore no longer fit for purpose.

The most recent revaluation came into effect in April 2017 and according to research by Altus Group, a rates adviser, they found the average rates bill for department stores in England and Wales was up 26.6 per cent in 2018/19. In contrast, rates for some online retailers dropped during the same period. ASOS and Shop Direct for example, are paying less on their distribution centres this year than last, while, according to Altus, Amazon paid just 0.7 per cent more.

The reason for this anomaly can be found in the fact that rates generally increased in city centres whilst they decreased in rural areas. It is no coincidence that this is where many of the online players' distribution centres are to be found. But shouldn't these be taxed in exactly the same way as High Street brick and mortar retailers? Both are delivering direct to the consumer. Taxing both on the value of the property makes no sense. As consumers we generally don't get to see the inside of an Amazon warehouse, however we shop with them in just the same way as we do if we walk into a shop on the high street. It's merely a different (some would say the same) delivery channel.

Tesco boss Dave Lewis has been particularly vocal of late in his opposition to the current business rates (Tesco is one of the UK's largest ratepayers with an annual business rates bill of around £700m) however he is not alone. Chairman of John Lewis, Sir Charlie Mayfield has seen the business rates tax for its flagship Oxford Street store rise by 57% from £12.68m to £19.91m under last year's revaluation. And this is not a new call to reform business rates, as long ago as August 2015, he told the Telegraph: "Business rates bills have continued to rise when property values have fallen. Reforming the rates system would be a welcome boost for retailers and help drive investment in training and technology". The British Retail Consortium have long championed a reform of the outdated business rates.

Whilst the call for change gets louder, as recent as July this year, Chancellor Philip Hammond was moved to say that the review of business rates in 2016 found "no consensus on an alternative base". However, a glimpse of hope was given last week by business secretary Greg Clark at the Tory party conference when he told a fringe group that business rates could change as "one way" of recognising the role played by high street retailers. But just as Nero was accused of 'fiddling while Rome burns' the chances of a business rates reform in the foreseeable future appear slim whilst all eyes are focused on Brussels. Let's hope that once our decree absolute comes through, we will still have a High Street to save.

Why The Budget Does Virtually Nothing For UK Retailers

First published in Forbes 29 October 2018

Almost as eagerly awaited as Black Friday or Cyber Monday, it's something which comes around once every autumn and this year's was anticipated even more so by the nation's beleaguered retailers. The 2018 Budget was announced today by Chancellor Philip Hammond but for those hoping for some relief, they were in for a big disappointment. The narrative has been one of struggling retail businesses but that is to paint a very one-dimensional picture. The issue facing bricks & mortar businesses has been the relentless onslaught by the online giants and the pure and simple fact is that the odds are heavily stacked against them.

Business rates

Stay with me and I'll try to explain the nub of the problem. The current system of business rates in the UK was introduced in 1990 and taxes any business on the 'rateable' value of the property; in other words, the tax is calculated based on the revenue generated if the property were rented. All well and good; a level playing field if you like. Except that in 1990, Amazon (to use an example) was still five years away, in other words, the system of taxation by which retail businesses are still obliged to comply with was created years before e-commerce and online shopping had ever been envisaged. Fast forward to 2018, with online pureplay retail business having huge out of town warehouses paying a pittance in business rates owing to the relatively low rateable value of their premises and you begin to appreciate the issue.

Why retailers will be up in arms

Despite much lobbying, especially on the part of the British Retail Consortium, the Budget did little to address this huge anomaly. The large global digital giants are hardly likely to be worried by the announcement with effect from April 2020 of a new 'Digital Services Tax'. Targeted at the revenue they raise from UK operations, it is anticipated to raise a (relatively) paltry £400m per annum. What is needed is a regeneration of growth and prosperity not just in our cities but especially in our towns up and down the country where it is the larger retail chains which drive footfall and therefore, in turn, benefit the whole High Street. The agenda is completely misplaced and this Budget demonstrates a fundamental lack of understanding of not just retail but the critical role it plays in our civic lives. A large out of town warehouse taking online orders and delivering direct to consumers is a retail business in exactly the same way as a store on the High Street; ergo both should be taxed in exactly the same manner. Until that level playing field is created, we should expect to see many more retail businesses shuttering stores or going out of business.

Retail 2019: Time To Get Back To Basics

First published in Forbes 9 November 2018

I thought I knew retail; maybe you thought you did too? Well, maybe it's time for a reality check. Because today, as we know, 20th century physical retail is under fire like never before. Faced with threats from all sides, but especially from online, it must focus on doing what the e-commerce techno whizzkids can't; namely delivering good old-fashioned face to face retailing based on an intimate knowledge of the customer. Customer experience is great but above all makes me feel wanted, valued.

Retail is everywhere and the very meaning of what it is to be a retailer is constantly being redefined but I would argue that to find retail at its purest you need to venture somewhere other than the e-commerce giants, the huge shopping malls and the out of town retail parks. Independent retailers are a different breed to the chains, they are independent for a reason and with this comes great autonomy, a liberating factor which even the best chains find hard to replicate.

One such example is Bettahomes which I write about in part three, suffice to say that his store typifies the very human nature of retail. Online is easy and convenient and is only getting better and better - especially when it comes to fulfilment; but it can never replace the deeply intimate human interaction which only comes with great physical, face to face retailing. We are all human and what we increasingly seek is to have great relationships with retailers and brands, ones which keep us coming back again and again and again. And that means knowing us, knowing our likes, dislikes, wants and needs. And it is the small independent retailers who are able to achieve this by building relationships with their customers.

Knowing and looking after the customer with a laser focus on service and doing what is right for the customer. This is the language that every retailer uses but how many actually put it into practice day in day out? Retail is undergoing unprecedented change and the threats to the old 20th-century model are many. Stores and especially, independent stores, are the lifeblood of towns up and down the country and they cannot be allowed to die out; our communities need them far too much for that to happen.

It's time to realize that we need retail to thrive, it's time to celebrate being a nation of shopkeepers, it's time to get back to basics. After all, getting back to basics has never been so key to survival.

A Brexit Boxset And Why It Is Such An Uncertain Time For Retail

First published in Forbes 16 November 2018

Are you sitting comfortably? Well, I'll begin. Once upon a time, there was something called the Maastricht Treaty and this created the European Union. All 28 member countries lived happily ever after in their new club as they now had Brussels there to look after them. Except that one member wasn't such a happy member after all. And so, it came to pass that this unhappy member decided that it wanted to leave. And almost overnight, Brexit! was created.

Now firmly established as one of the U.K.'s most popular soap operas, as I write, the latest episode titled 'Draft Withdrawal Agreement' is on our screens. Starring Prime Minister Theresa May, it is proving to be a great success with plenty of plot twists to keep us on the edge of our seats. But understanding the language used is proving to be somewhat of a challenge.

Understanding Brexit - not the work of a moment

Hard Brexit, soft Brexit, backstop, backstop to the backstop, Article 50, Chequers Plan.....it goes on and on and it's hardly surprising that most of us are left completely baffled by the whole thing. Just who are the good guys and who are the bad guys? It's increasingly difficult to tell. Jump to the real world (if that indeed is actually what it is and not some sad parody of The Truman Show) and back in June 2016, the result of the referendum was celebrated as a victory, the U.K. would take back its sovereignty and be free to strike trade deals with whoever it jolly well-liked instead of being tied to the European Union.

In July 2017, then International Trade Secretary, Liam Fox, declared that securing a free trade deal with the European Union should be "one of the easiest in human history". I've got news for you Liam, wind forward to November 2018, just 5 months before the date the U.K. is due to leave the European Union, and things look decidedly different. Ministers resigning, a Government in turmoil, any deal better than no deal and a Prime Minister stoically clinging to the dying embers of her power, ironically uniting both Leave and Remain supporters in condemning what they feel is a bad deal with Brussels.

Retail reeling

But putting the pantomime politics to one side for a moment, just what impact is all this having on retail? Retailers and consumers alike being locked into a perverse kind of limbo, not knowing quite what is going to happen next. For businesses across all sectors, it is a time of great uncertainty; and business does NOT like uncertainty. For retailers 'the perfect storm' is now a reality: low consumer confidence, rising costs through tax and staff costs, a weak pound meaning the cost of goods imported has increased, competition from online and now on top of which, the seemingly insurmountable challenge of Brexit. Casting its shadow in Dickensian style - truly the ghost of backstop past, present and future.

The fear is that the deal on the table won't get through Parliament, the implications of which could result in an exit from the EU with no deal. The nightmare this conjures is of the primary trade route between Dover and Calais grinding to a halt through the need for physical customs checks. This is the primary concern of retailers and consumers alike and is leading to consumer stockpiling in the event of just such a scenario.

Food supply chain under threat

And whilst politicians try to assuage the public by saying that supermarkets will keep stocking their shelves in the event of a no deal Brexit, one leading supermarket CEO told me that this is absolute nonsense. "It's not as if we have any spare warehouse capacity," he said, adding, "besides, the entire supply chain is built on a just in time model. Fruit picked in Spain on a Monday is on our shelves by Thursday." Should a no deal Brexit occur, the U.K. would be forced to trade with the EU with higher World Trade Organisation tariffs, which would hit the retail sector hard. - Moody's Credit Ratings

So, for supermarkets, the prospect of produce rotting at our ports is a very real one in the event of a no deal. However, it's not just the impact on the food supply chain at our ports which is of concern, Co-op boss Steve Murrells said, "We're worried that in the season of harvest and picking, farming relies on migrant labour and if the wrong outcome prevails there is going to be a real shortage of people to pick the crops" Former Sainsbury's boss Justin King had this to say; "I think when you see that something is not going to be a good outcome, then you have to keep fighting for an alternative", adding that the current situation makes it difficult for retailers to make any sort of decisions.

Leading credit rating agency Moody's also warns that a no deal Brexit would represent a serious threat to retail and plunge the country into recession. And the growing anxiety and uncertainty around Brexit are mirrored in the retail sales figures for October, which according to the Office for National Statistics (ONS) were down

0.5% in October against a forecast of a rise of 0.2%. As we enter the crucial peak trading period, uncertainty and low consumer confidence are things retailers can definitely do without. They, like all of us, wait with fevered anticipation for the next episode of Brexit! - will Parliament accept the deal? Will Theresa stay or will she go? Stay tuned for the next nail-biting episode of Brexit! the gripping story of a country tearing itself apart.

Why Brexit Is Proving Disastrous For Retail

First published in Forbes 21 January 2019

Tick, tock, tick, tock goes the Brexit clock, and with each passing day a little more misery is heaped upon the U.K.'s besieged retail sector. I first wrote about Brexit in my **Forbes post** in mid-November, and at that time we were unclear of exactly what outcome to expect, and that was just over four months from the deadline of March 29th, 2019. Now, as I write; absolutely nothing, I repeat nothing, has changed. The 'meaningful vote' was held in Parliament on January 15th and as expected, Theresa May's deal was defeated. However, no-one quite expected the magnitude of the loss, the biggest in Parliamentary history.

In normal times, this would have resulted in her resignation; but these are far from normal times. Stay she did and not only that but the next chapter to be played out is scheduled for January 29th when we shall have another 'meaningful vote' in Parliament. And guess what? Nothing's changed. She will present her plan B to Parliament but in reality, plan B is no different to plan A; the ultimate definition of madness?

Can retail wait any longer?

Now you may be reading this with growing incredulity, wondering just how democracy could possibly operate like this. For the good citizens of the U.K. that incredulity and subsequent mockery of both the Government and Parliament have given way to rising anger that is dividing the country like never before.
And all the while, retail continues to suffer.

According to the British Retail Consortium, retail endured its **worst Christmas** in a decade. And not for the first time, one of the primary reasons for the decline is the uncertainty and fear of the very real prospect of the U.K. crashing out of Europe with a no deal Brexit. BRC chief executive Helen Dickinson was moved to say: "Squeezed consumers chose not to splash out this Christmas, with retail sales growth stalling for the first time in 28 months". The perfect storm is rapidly becoming *the* most perfect storm. And sadly, some retail businesses simply won't survive.

Cash-starved through falling sales, margins eroded by heavier and heavier discounting, increases in business rates just around the corner, the crisis of consumer confidence is having a disastrous effect. It brings to mind a conversation I had with a senior executive at MFI, just days before its collapse into administration in November 2008, the business was living hand to mouth just trying to pay suppliers and landlords. In the end, it proved too much.

Arcadia, the fashion group owned by Sir Philip Green is the latest to come under intense pressure, closing over two hundred stores in the last two years and seeing sales dip below £2 billion for the first time in eight years. The embattled retailer saying that there was 'great uncertainty' caused by Brexit. And they're not alone. In the run-up to Christmas, Hamleys blamed Brexit for a staggering 500% drop in profits. Similarly, in December, shares at Bonmarché **plummeted** more than two fifths as it issued its second profit warning in three months, citing 'unprecedented' trading conditions and Brexit uncertainty.

Meanwhile, Marks and Spencer are the latest to announce further store closures as their battle on the high street continues. The list goes on, and all the while, instead of becoming clearer as we approach the March deadline, the Brexit fog rolls in unabated, ever thicker and thicker. Meanwhile, the Brexit clock goes tick, tock, tick, tock.

MPs Report On The High Street Falls Short

First published in Forbes 22 February 2019

Six months in the making, involving retailers, town planners, local authorities, academics, and industry experts, the 'High Streets and town centres in 2030' report by the Housing, Communities and Local Government Committee was published this week. The report concluded that 'wide reforms' are needed to secure the future of our high streets and town centres. That much we knew, the question, however, remains, how to address the issue?

On that point, the report refers to 'dated policies' and that an 'unfair tax regime must be reformed to create an environment that will allow high streets and town centres to flourish in the future'. It calls on the Government to 'initiate reform in key planning and taxation areas, including the options of an Online Sales Tax and reforms to business rates, to allow high streets to adapt to changing demand, and compete with online retailers such as Amazon on a level playing field'.

All very laudable and there is now almost common agreement that the creation of a level playing field is required in order that all retail businesses can compete fairly and equitably. Chair of the Housing, Communities and Local Government Committee, Clive Betts MP commented: "In recent years, high streets and town centres have faced extremely challenging times. We have seen the collapse of a number of well-known, national high street chains, with many more undergoing restructuring or being bought out. The growth of online shopping has profoundly changed retail in the UK, and the knock-on impact on high streets has been stark"

It is likely that the heyday of the high street primarily as a retail hub is at an end. However, this need not be its death knell. Local authorities must get to grips with the fact that their town centres need to change; they need to innovate, setting out a long-term strategy for renewal, reconfiguring the town centre and finding new ways of using buildings and encouraging new independent retailers. Dated planning policy must be reformed to reflect the needs of modern high streets and town centres. Business rates must be made fair. They are currently stacking the odds against businesses with a high street presence and this must end. Tax reforms are needed to level the playing field between online and high street retailers, and we urge the Government to investigate all the options in this area, including an Online Sales Tax. Local authorities must have the foresight to develop evolving strategies tailored to the needs of their local communities and drive the large-scale transformation needed. Central government must give them the powers, and back them financially, to allow them to put this into practice.

The real issue

What of course the report should be advocating is complete scrapping of the existing business rates system which was introduced in 1990, years before online shopping was ever dreamt of. Consider that in today's consumer-led world, a warehouse off the M40 in Oxfordshire is delivering directly to the consumer in just the same way as a shop on London's Oxford Street, the only difference being that they are currently taxed in hugely different ways. Levying a 'success tax' on the online retail businesses does not address this fundamental anomaly.

Nor for that matter does the £675 million future high streets fund announced in the October 2018 budget; to put that in context, in 2017 Amazon reportedly spent $23 billion on research and development alone. A further complexity to the equation occurs when one considers just what constitutes an online purchase these days? Where in other words does the sales attribution belong when an item is purchased online but only after the customer went in-store first to showroom the product or indeed, vice versa? It's only when one really begins to delve into the shopping patterns and behaviour of consumers today that one realizes the fallacy of an Online Sales Tax.

The time to act is now

Whilst a worthy addition to the debate, the report ultimately falls short and perhaps more importantly, whether you agree with that statement or not, the bigger issue is whether it will attract an audience and stimulate action or whether it will simply become a Whitehall dust magnet? I'm tempted to say time will tell, but of course, that would be wrong because if there's one thing we do not have, it's time.

The time, so to speak, to act is now. Not tomorrow, not next week, not next month, else we risk sleep-walking into a dystopian future, the likes of which none of us, I would venture, would be happy to leave as our legacy.

Arcadia And An Austin Allegro Have More In Common Than You Might Think

First published in Forbes 8 June 2019

Let's be honest, cars in the '70s and '80s weren't particularly good. I can still recall the dawn chorus of coaxing recalcitrant engines into life on a cold winter's morning. They had a habit of simply stopping when you least expected it and needed constant maintenance. Amongst the worst were those emerging from the Longbridge factory in Birmingham. If you've ever owned an Austin Allegro you'll know what I mean. It was a truly awful contraption; there's a good reason why so few are still in existence. Most simply rotted away.

Now, you might be thinking, what's this got to do with retail? Well, actually, it's got everything to do with retail. Because cars, not dissimilar to stores, need maintaining. This is why your car has a service schedule. It's not because the dealer just likes to see you and provide you with coffee once a year, it's there for a good reason. Because cars just happen to have a lot of moving parts, parts which, over time, wear out and need replacing. This costs money.

And there's more. Here in the U.K. every car over three years old - yes, just three years - needs to be inspected to make sure it's safe and roadworthy. It's called a MOT. And it costs money too. For car owners, running a car means you have to spend money on it from time to time in order that it continues to be reliable and performs not only as it should but to the level which is required of it. So, cars need maintenance if they are to keep going. Well, stores are not dissimilar. Unfortunately, one owner of his once gleaming pride and joy appears to have neglected his maintenance schedule and is now paying the price.

Which is why Arcadia is not unlike an Austin Allegro, and is currently on the brink of breaking down. Permanently. Only, instead of the AA or RAC coming out to fix it, they have their creditors circling, deciding whether it should be written off as being uneconomical to keep on the road. Because, for some strange reason, the owner of Arcadia didn't feel that his vehicle required any maintenance. Preferring to simply continue to enjoy it and skip the associated costs.

But of course, that can only continue for so long until things start to fail and the consequential cost of repair starts to increase and in the worst cases, simply isn't viable. In the case of Arcadia, the owner is currently facing a repair bill of some £385 million and the figure is rising all the time. And it appears that the particular garage he's taken his vehicle to isn't especially enamoured by the way he's been treating his once pride and joy. The exterior is looking worn and the interior is pretty shabby in many places. Years of neglect have taken their toll on a once gleaming appearance. Not unreasonably, the garage this owner has taken his vehicle to, wants to do a proper job in order to ensure that he continues to enjoy many more trouble-free years out of it. This is costing him more than he originally anticipated. Which is unfortunate. All this is a salutary tale. And the moral of the story? Keep up with your service schedule, it's there for a reason.

PART SIX: OLD RETAIL, NEW TRICKS

The rise of new retail, which is taking over, the changing of the guard if you like, is happening right in front of us. Harry Selfridge was way ahead of his time when he said that he wanted his store to be somewhere where people wish to gather, to socialise, to spend time together. Ironically, this is being touted as the future of retail. Whereas the philosophy has been around for over a hundred years. It's just that new retail businesses get this and are embracing it whereas old retail businesses cannot migrate away from the sell first culture.

Old retail has been around for decades, opening store after store, running the business in a particular fashion. Vertical, siloed, top down, command and control from the centre, running the business on a cost budget basis where sales are the only thing that matters. On top of this, the means by which success was measured was determined in the same fashion: sales per square foot, sales per employee – the key performance indicators (KPIs) of every retail business. Except that things were changing. Fundamentally. And in ways that old retail could never imagine. It had been coming for a while but it was two events just over ten years ago that really crystalized the transformation which was taking place.

The first was in January 2007 when Steve Jobs went on stage at MacWorld in California and announced the launch of a new phone, a new iPod (remember them?) and a new internet exploration device. The audience were wowed, they had expected the launch of one new device but here was three! He repeated what he'd just said and there were ripples in the audience – some had cottoned on. He then repeated it for a third time and this time cheering started to break out. Yes, you too have probably guessed it by now, this was the launch of the first iPhone. Just over ten years ago. Think of that for a moment and you begin to realise how rapidly we have come to shift our expectations. Why was this significant? Because for the first time, this gave us the power. This gave us, in this one device, the power to begin to have an influence and for our voices to be heard like never before. And in doing so it changed the very nature of the relationship we have with retailers. For decades, old retail had enjoyed a parent / child relationship with their customers – with them very much being the parent. The birth of the smartphone – and with it, social media – changed all that.

The second event occurred a little over a year later. This was the global financial crisis, prompted by the subprime crisis. How did the U.S. economy get to a point where in 2007, a full-on housing crisis began? It doesn't happen overnight. In the early-to-mid 2000s, interest rates on house payments were actually quite low. In what looked to be a solid economy after a brief early 2000s recession, more and more people with struggling credit were able to qualify for subprime mortgages with manageable rates, and happily acted on that. This sudden increase in subprime mortgages was due in part to the Federal Reserve's decision to significantly lower the Federal funds rate to spur growth. People who couldn't afford homes or get approved for loans were suddenly qualifying for subprime loans and choosing to buy, and American home ownership rose exponentially. Real estate purchases rose not only for subprime borrowers, but for well-off Americans as well. As prices rose and people expected a continuation of that, investors who got burned by the dot com bubble of the early 2000s and needed a replacement in their portfolio started investing in real estate. Housing prices were rising rapidly, and the number of subprime mortgages given out was rising even more. By 2005, some began to fear that this was a housing bubble. From 2004-2006, the Federal Reserve raised the interest rate over a dozen times in an attempt to slow this down and avoid serious inflation. By the end of 2004, the interest rate was 2.25%; by mid-2006 it was 5.25%.

This was unable to stop the inevitable. The bubble burst. 2005 and 2006 saw the housing market crash back down to earth. Subprime mortgage lenders began laying thousands of employees off, if not filing for bankruptcy or shutting down entirely. The biggest and most high-profile casualty of the fall-out from this was Lehman Brothers. Founded in 1847 they were the fourth largest investment bank in the United States. In 2008, they filed for bankruptcy. The shockwaves were felt around the world. In the U.K. history shows us that we entered a prolonged period of enforced 'austerity' which we still experience to an extent to this day.

This had the effect that as consumers our attitudes fundamentally changed. We became far more frugal, we became smarter at seeking out value and bargains – increasingly using that smartphone in our pockets to do so. Where once the discounters such as Aldi, Lidl, Poundland and Primark - to name a few - were largely the preserve of particular demographics, now we began to see BMWs, Mercedes and Audis in Lidl car parks. And with all this came the birth of the savvy consumer. And our shopping habits changed forever. It was the introduction of the smartphone that gave us the means and the financial crisis the incentive, to become who we are today. The implications of this are profound and one of the prime reasons why old retail is now struggling.

What this resulted in was not just a smarter consumer but a far more demanding one. Think of your own shopping behaviour now as opposed to ten or fifteen years ago. Or especially to that of your parents. Different isn't it? One thing which you probably lack in any great abundance when it comes to which brands you choose to spend your money with is loyalty. I imagine that you will have your favourites but that you will quite happily migrate from one to the other to another frequently. And not only that, but if a once favourite brand fails to perform in exactly that way you want or expect then you'll drop them in a heartbeat. This is the impatience, the lack of tolerance that we display now as compared to in the past. It took old retail longer to realise this than its new upstart competitors and once behind it is extremely difficult to catch up. Because once you think you've caught up, when you get there, it's only to find that the goal has shifted. Forever out of reach, this is consigning many who reside in old retail to the ranks of bit-part players.

Old retail needs to learn new tricks. And that is not just me saying that. At the launch of the World Retail Congress last year, Lord Stuart Rose was damning in his indictment of old retail and that they need to "throw away the rulebook as it is no longer fit for purpose". This is unlikely to happen for a while. Not until the current thirty-something millennials get into positions of influence within organisations will we see real change. This is because the large majority are run by a certain demographic. Male fifty-somethings who have been in retail all their lives and know nothing else. Their decisions informed by their own experiences of what good once used to look like, not realising that yesterday's good is today's failure.

If you've got young or teenage children, have you ever stopped to observe the way they use their smartphones, especially to communicate, to socialise, to engage and to shop? Different isn't it? Different in so many ways. And it is this mentality, this expectation and this way of operating which new retail understands and can tap into. Old retail must learn new tricks as rapidly as possible and realise that there are other ways of working. The alternative is sadly being played out on virtually every high street in the country.

Start-ups Continue To Innovate Delivery Options For Retailers

First published in Retail Week 20 March 2015

Two days, over 100 speakers, more than a 1,000 delegates – Retail Week Live was again the highlight in the retail calendar this year. Bigger and better than ever, this was a landmark event in retail. Never before has the pace of change been so frenetic, never before has the future looked so uncertain. In the words of retail bosses, the retail climate today is "challenging" and "threatening". We heard about failing fast, daily release cycles, experimentation, personalisation, working with start-ups, click-and-collect; in short this felt like a conference of its time. We heard many leading retailers describe how click-and-collect is driving their business, how they are introducing it, how it creates challenges for them (supply chain and in-store especially) and we heard how click-and-collect is not only driving double-digit sales growth, but that it is embedded within their business models. But surely click-and-collect is but a stepping stone? A stepping stone to something more convenient for the consumer.

After all, why would we want to order online and then have to collect from a store? Unless of course we have a reason to visit the store, click-and-collect appears to have been initially a consumer-led service which is now rapidly becoming a retail strategy to drive footfall in store and thus take advantage of upsell and cross sell. What if we could have click-and-deliver? Order online (or in store for that matter) and have the goods delivered to our home. Nothing new in that you might say. But at Retail Week Live this year there was a new addition; the Innovation Campus. Run along the Dragons' Den principle, it showcased more than a dozen inspiring start-ups, all pitching their retail innovation products. And tucked away in a corner of all this was, for me, the most important and significant aspect of the entire conference.

Game-changer

The secure plastic box known as a Pelipod sat there pretty anonymously, but the significance of having a secure box outside our homes, along with all our various recycling bins, should not be underestimated. No more trips to the local depot or Post Office when we find the ubiquitous card on the doormat, no more deliveries tossed over the garden fence, or with the neighbours and especially, no more waiting in for that delivery that never happened. With this we are liberated from being tied to a delivery and that is game-changing.

And with returns handled just as easily, for all those retailers building a business model around click-and-collect I would urge caution. The consumer drives the pace and type of change and this would seem to be an ideal candidate. As the two keynotes from Dixons Carphone boss Seb James at the opening of the conference and Sainsbury's chief Mike Coupe at the close both echoed: "adapt or die".

Crack It With Cognitive

First published in Retail Reflections 18 May 2017

Think of that last significant purchase you made. New laptop? A holiday? New sofa? At this time of year maybe it was a new barbecue. Now do something I'd imagine you rarely do (consciously that is). Think of the process you went through from first thinking about that new barbecue or laptop right up to purchasing it. Straightforward? Doubtful. It wouldn't be at all surprising if the journey was not only complex but may have played out over a protracted period of time, involved multiple interactions with multiple brands and was a mix of online and in-store research and browsing. It might also have involved asking friends and family for their experiences and recommendations. Sounds familiar?

In the consumer environment of today nothing is straightforward, nothing is predictable and everything is up for grabs. So why is this important?

Finding a logical solution

What puzzle could be more tricky, more complex for the human brain to comprehend than 3D chess as played by Mr Spock and Captain Kirk? Well, how about mapping the customer journey? The path to purchase, has for many years been the subject of intense study amongst retailers. But guess what? Instead of getting easier, it is more complex than ever and an understanding of it is rapidly receding far out of sight. Predictable? Forget it. It may just be shopping but the complexity is now such that retailers struggle to keep up – to understand their customers' preferences, indeed to even grasp why they behave the way they do.

That smartphone in our pockets not only gives us incredible choice, it gives us incredible influence and, dare we say it, incredible power. It allows us to flit from one brand to another with impunity. Fuelled by the still vivid memory of austerity now amplified by the uncertainty of Brexit, we are constantly seeking out better offers, better deals – better experiences. And not only that, but our expectations have never been higher than they are now.

Data, data everywhere

With so much of shoppers' behaviour unpredictable, with so many different influences on us and our own promiscuous shopping behaviour, how can brands possibly understand the customer journey of today?

Most use some form of analytics and many have reached levels of impressive maturity but they all have one major drawback. Traditional analytics rely on being pre-programmed and therefore can only act and analyse based on that pre-programmed input. Not only that but it can only recognise structured data. In other words, all the unstructured data such as pictures, video and news articles is largely invisible. Now consider this: there is at present more than 1 zettabyte (ZB) of data online and this will rise to over 40ZB by 2020. To make that a little more real, it would take you 152m years to watch 1ZB of data in HD video and traditional computer analysis can only see 20% of that.

Cognitive

Think of all those pictures and video you and your children are uploading to Facebook, Instagram, Twitter, YouTube, Snapchat every day. And now think how much about your life, your family, your hobbies, your preferences you are sharing with the world – your digital footprint. And yet the world isn't listening. Now think of a world where not only is all that data being recognised, it is also being interpreted and acted upon whilst all the time learning about you. To the point where your needs and wants can be accurately predicted and relevant offers for goods and services presented to you completely in context. Seems far-fetched? Welcome to the world of cognitive computing and machine learning.

Think of it as your very own Einstein right there at your side being able to constantly update and learn, interpreting not only your digital output but within the context of all the data in the world around you. The future is here now and the consumer revolution we are currently witnessing has never been more profound. The only question remaining is how long will it take retail brands to grasp this and act upon it?

Enhanced Automation And Why Our Skies Won't Be Filled With Drones

First published in Retail Reflections 1 June 2018

Mention automation in the supply chain and for many of us this conjures up an Orwellian vision of a future where humans are subservient to our robotic masters, the sorcerer's apprentice if you will. And whilst the reality might be a little less dramatic, there is no doubt that the rapid pace of change is sweeping through all aspects of retail, and in particular, supply chain and logistics. Alongside their retail cousins visual merchandising and buying, stock replenishment and purchase order management may on the surface, have limited appeal.

However, the truth today is rather different. It's a fact that inventory management and technology were simply made for each other; just think for a moment of a world where the Internet of Things (IoT) and radio frequency identification (RFID) allow you to know where every piece of stock is at any one time, in real time, without ever having to move from your seat. If visibility of stock is proving a challenge it might be time to invest in automated inventory management Total 100% visibility of inventory; the retail holy grail? The good news is that it's available today.

Automated stock replenishment combined with automated purchase order management creates a powerful, accurate automatic replenishment engine.
Add to that the power of Artificial Intelligence (AI) and machine learning and one can begin to imagine that utopian dream. As far back as 2014, PwC coined the term 'Total Retail' to describe: "A unified brand story across all channels, that promises a consistently superior customer experience and an integrated back office operating model with agile and innovative technology" Seems straightforward when seen through the lens four years later however, according to Deloitte in their 2018 Global Chief Procurement Officer survey; "65% of procurement leaders having limited or no visibility beyond their tier 1 suppliers".

Anything everywhere……anytime

Once seen as very much a back-office support operation, inventory management is now at the heart of all retail operations. Automated stock replenishment and purchase order management are now vital to success. A look at successful online retailers such as ASOS, Shop Direct and Boohoo reveal why. Clear and transparent, rather than opaque visibility of inventory combined with one view of product across the business allows not only for great availability but less stock-outs, mark downs and crucially, the ability to constantly introduce new products. In the case of ASOS this equates to 5,000 new items every week. This last is especially critical for today's demanding consumer. Here's why.

Great expectations

It might not have been what Charles Dickens had in mind when he wrote about the orphan Pip in his 13th novel, however it is a fact that our expectations as consumers are now higher than ever before and what's more they are on a relentless quest for better and better service. To understand why stock replenishment and purchase order management are so critical to success in today's retail environment, first we need to understand ourselves – the consumer.

Think of a time when you experienced great retail service – whether it was online, in-store or a combination of both. Chances are the memory of it will last a long time; in fact, psychologists tell us that the memory of the experience is more powerful than the experience itself. Except that today, as consumers, we have a number of different character traits which, whilst they may have always been there, that latency has now been awakened. What characterises today's consumer? Impatience mixed with high expectation makes for an insatiable appetite for the next best thing, the next best experience. Each time, the bar is being raised and nowhere is this more important than in a retailer's ability to deliver.

We are rapidly entering an age where the brand will be defined not by price or product but by its ability to deliver. Automation of inventory management, using AI and machine learning to predict demand and provide visibility of stock wherever it is in the supply chain, will herald a completely new era in retail. No more one-hour delivery slots, we will expect delivery within the hour – wherever we happen to be. Whether we are on holiday, at a concert, a conference, a sports event – or in urgent need of a key ingredient for that important dinner party – whatever it happens to be, we will expect to be able to order and have it delivered within the hour. This is already happening.

Founded in 2014, Urb.it are currently in Stockholm, Paris and London; through digitising local retailers and utilising a fleet of couriers known as 'urbers' they promise to deliver wherever you are within the hour. The skies may not about to be filled with drones but enhanced automation in inventory management is driving a new capability which is quenching that insatiable thirst. The future is happening now; can you afford to be left out?

How Social Media Influence Will Increasingly Affect Retail Success

First published in Retail Week 25 August 2015

Retail is a social activity so it is no surprise that the industry and consumers alike have embraced social media as part of the experience. According to a McKinsey Global Institute study, 85% of consumer and retail companies are using social technologies for marketing compared to 66% of companies in other industries. Social media tools give retailers the opportunity to personalise the consumer-seller experience, a recent Hootsuite study found. This is a vital point yet to be accepted by many retailers who view social media as just another form of marketing to their customers. As consumers, we are increasingly seeking more personalised, relevant engagement with retail brands.

More than ever, we are asked to divulge personal data about ourselves – remember the last time you wanted to use free WiFi in-store? – and in return we expect that retail brands will engage with us in a relevant, meaningful and timely manner. However, in order to do so, retailers must have a single view of each and every one of their customers. Sadly, in most cases, this is still a little way off but it represents an enormous opportunity. Which means that today, we are merely scratching the surface of the power of social media in retail.

Customer emphasis

Most retailers simply use social media as a means to market and capture feedback, and this is unlikely to change. Some, however, appreciate that in order to harness the power of social media, instead of mere platitudes, they must actually put the customer at the very centre of their organisation. Witness the pioneering restructure at House of Fraser which has created a unified customer insight team bringing together the retailer's brand, CRM, product and multichannel functions for the first time.

And social media will play an increasingly vital role in this, going beyond simply listening as it moves towards putting the customer at the heart of a retail business. Consumers are more likely to shop with a retailer they know and trust, but the path to purchase experience has to be positive and engaging at the same time. Social media plays a large part in this relationship with the consumer but is under-utilised by many retailers owing to a fear of misuse or negative publicity.

Social impact

The proliferation of smartphones gives rise to another reason why social interaction is key to the success of a retail brand; consumers are able to access information, peer reviews, research products and brands, check prices all while on the go. Before even entering a store, 62% of millennial shoppers already know what they want to buy through prior online research, according to Bazaarvoice. And 84% of them say consumer-written content on brand sites influences what they buy. In the next few years, largely driven by consumer demands and expectations, social and retail will become one, such that social will be the primary source for engaging with customers, driving sales and increasing brand awareness – to the point where social influence will play a leading role in the deals, bargains and discounts we each receive from retailers. Have you checked your Klout score recently? It may be time to start paying attention to it if you want to grab all the best bargains.

Why Jimmy Choo Is A Good Fit For Michael Kors

First published in Retail Week 26 July 2017

The news that Michael Kors is to buy Jimmy Choo for £896m should come as no surprise. Back in 2015 when it was announced that Michael Kors competitor Coach was to purchase luxury footwear brand Stuart Weitzman, there would have been much gnashing of teeth at the Michael Kors headquarters in New York. This would have become a wail in May this year when it was announced that Coach was buying luxury handbag brand Kate Spade. However, that will have dissipated now with the purchase of Jimmy Choo. This option was opened up by the decision of Michael Kors' German owners, the JAB Holding Company, to migrate from the luxury market to focus on their other businesses, such as coffee brand Douwe Egberts. On the news of the deal, shares in Jimmy Choo jumped 17% while Michael Kors' share price recovered slightly after a rollercoaster 12 months.

Luxury appeal

So, what's going on here? Why are luxury brands being snapped up? The answer is simple and lies in two things: the global marketplace and the brand itself. Take Michael Kors; a combination of discounting, too many stores, brand uncertainty on the part of its customers leading to declining revenues and a share price which fell by nearly 60% in the last 12 months. As shoppers are increasingly drawn to the extremes of the market, both discount and luxury, Michael Kors was caught in the middle. A potentially fatal position to be in which was not sustainable. So something had to be done.

Clear brand values

In March this year, Jimmy Choo announced record revenues and the following month it indicated that it was seeking a new owner. For Michael Kors, an opportunity to not only reposition but, in Jimmy Choo, an opportunity to exploit new avenues of growth globally. Once seen as a luxury brand, Michael Kors has systematically diluted its brand through promotions and discounting to the point where customers were no longer willing to pay full price. Jimmy Choo however, is very clear on where the brand sits, there is no ambiguity – if your budget only stretches to £100, don't bother. It inhabits a much more rarefied place and customers know it. It's a perfect example of the need to understand a brand and what it stands for and, conversely, what happens when that view becomes blurred.

Why Christmas Ads Must Pass The Goosebump Test

First published in Retail Week 16 November 2016

Retailers' Christmas campaigns need a few essential ingredients to stand out. What do John Lewis, Aldi, Lidl, Waitrose, Sainsbury's, M&S and Tesco all have in common? Answer: in the last week they have all released their 2016 Christmas TV ads to an expectant audience. Yes, 'tis the season to ooh and ah, feel the goosebumps and maybe shed a tear or two. It is always fascinating to see the different interpretations of what Christmas means brought to life on screen. While John Lewis has rightly been the benchmark for many years, this year it perhaps been eclipsed. And some retailers' ads, frankly, probably deserved to stay on the cutting room floor. So what makes a great retail Christmas ad? I'd argue that to be impactful, there are five characteristics that all successful ones should possess.

Brand engagement

Any successful TV ad campaign needs to not only be clear about the brand but most importantly what the brand stands for, and never is that more important than at Christmas. In other words, the brand must strive to become a part of someone's Christmas memories (many still recall John Lewis's 'Man on the Moon') and in this way the connection is made.

Emotional attachment

Which brings us nicely to the emotional attachment – especially at Christmas when our emotions are more receptive than ever to suggestion. For many people, Christmas is a time for reflection and sharing. The best ads exploit this with images that stir these feelings and this has certainly been a recurring theme this year with John Lewis, M&S and Waitrose all pressing these buttons.

Ability to inspire

Against all this is the backdrop of a much tougher retail environment where consumer loyalty is a thing of the past, and shoppers are ever more savvy and unpredictable in their behaviour. The Christmas ad is an opportunity for retailers to claw back custom. Let's face it, most people are seeking a little gift inspiration.

Music

Music stirs the soul and no more so is this evident than when a great soundtrack provides the canvas for a Christmas ad. Whether it be British newcomers The Vaults with their version of 'One Day I'll Fly Away' (John Lewis) or Rachel Portman and 'With Love' (M&S), it's the music which stirs us as much as anything else.

The goosebump test

Last but by no means least, the goosebump test. Everybody has experienced it and if an ad has all the other characteristics listed here, it will surely pass this test. Whether it be the bouncing foxes, Mrs Claus welcoming her husband home, the robin reunited with his mate or even Kevin the carrot, if it passes the goosebump test then there can't be much wrong.

And which is my personal favourite? While I love Kevin the carrot from Aldi, this year the award has to go to M&S. Featuring Mrs Claus, 21st century technology and an emotionally charged soundtrack, it pretty much ticks all the boxes.

Embrace Change – And Do It Now

First published in Retail Reflections 5 April 2018

We are living through the biggest period of disruption and change ever to impact the retail industry. We hear it every week: profit warnings, CVA's and once great retail businesses going into administration; Darwinism on the High Street - if you will – is now a stark reality for us all. To try to make sense of all this, IBM and Retail Reflections hosted a retail roundtable dinner. Held at the Gherkin in London the event gathered a group of senior retailers to discuss the state of the High Street and much more. As Founder of DFS, Lord Kirkham put it: "Embrace change – and do it now". Held shortly after NRF in New York and more recently Retail Week Live in London, there was plenty to discuss. And emerging from both retail conferences were three stand out trends:

- Artificial Intelligence
- Role of the store
- Frictionless commerce

Artificial intelligence (AI) is perhaps the biggest and most significant change the retail industry has seen for decades and there was plenty of discussion around just what AI is and what AI isn't. And in a stark word of warning to all retailers, "If you haven't begun your AI journey yet, you'll never be able to catch up". There is a certain amount of irony in the fact that online continues to grab all the headlines and yet only accounts for around 15-17% of sales (depending on which part of the world you're in).

So, it seemed natural to discuss the role of the store which is now rapidly evolving from a place simply to keep the stock dry to the new battleground of retail where the experience is everything. And in this context, the ways in which physical can be merged with digital was the focus of much discussion. Those who are able to a) use an appropriate blend of technologies and b) create a seamless physical / digital in-store environment are those more likely to succeed.

Which brought us nicely to the 3rd key trend – that of frictionless commerce. It's long been known that the shopping journey needs to be easy and convenient but this is being acutely felt now – in an age where if your website takes more than a few seconds to load, you've lost that customer. Less tolerant, impatient, more demanding than ever before; the margins for error are at best slim if you are to attract and retain today's tech savvy consumer.

What trends will we see in 2018?

We concluded the evening with a literal roundtable; the subject? What trends are we likely to see in 2018? There were some interesting views. As expected, AI featured; it is pervasive in pretty much everything. Blockchain was another technology raised, beware estate agents – your days could be numbered; maybe a reinvention is required? Ease of checkout echoed the frictionless discussion and it is clear that the entire checkout / payment process will in future be transformed. There is clearly a shift in the ways that consumers wish to interact and whilst technology must be kept in its rightful place – unobtrusive, enabling rather than confusing – the right mix of technology is key to addressing shortcomings and failures. Final mile fulfilment was another topic discussed; now more important than ever before – a brand's ability to deliver whenever, wherever will largely come to define it. Supply chain flexibility enabled by inventory visibility is now vital for any retailer.

Conclusion

The sheer pace of change and innovation can at times be bewildering. For those retailers still clinging to the belief that past working practices will continue to work – a nasty shock is just around the corner. It's sometimes difficult to appreciate that what we are experiencing in 2018 is not just another trend but that we are living through a seismic revolution in retail. Old ways no longer work, are no longer relevant. It's time to throw away the rule book; retail is dead, long live retail.

Why The Time Is Now For The Forgotten Technology Of Retail

First published in Forbes 12 November 2018

According to Mark Roberti of the RFID Journal, it's generally believed that the roots of radio frequency identification technology can be traced back to World War II. Radio Frequency Identification (RFID) has come a long way since those days however its progress in retail has somewhat stagnated for the past 20 years; until now that is. Originally touted as a security device in order to lessen shrinkage (that's theft to you and I) it never really took off, largely down to cost implications. In the early 2000's, Walmart was the first big retailer to experiment with the new technology, which cost an astounding $1.50 per tag.

RFID tags today, however, are incredibly small and.......far less expensive; such that the cost is no longer an issue. But brick and mortar retailers aren't looking to RFID so much as an aid to lessen theft, there are other, even more, compelling reasons why they are now turning to it and the answer is somewhat perverse.

Inventory is king

In today's world, I just don't simply want it, I want it now and, oh by the way, I want it where I need it. So, for that new dress, that new jacket, that new shirt, it's not simply a question of having one in stock. You need to know where precisely that item is, at any given time. Always. How many times do you take a stock check? Twice a year? With RFID stock checks can be virtually continual, in other words, it provides the retailer with a view of where each individual stock item is at any stage in the supply chain. The rapid growth in online has therefore given rise for the need for retailers to have far better visibility of their stock; 65% just doesn't cut it any longer, this needs to be greater than 90% and this is what RFID can deliver.

And where a simple barcode can tell you, 'this is a $250 jacket in grey', an RFID tag can tell you 'this is a $250 jacket in grey, size medium, the one which was returned last week and it's just walking out the door'. According to Accenture in its 'Transforming Modern Retail' report from August 2018, 92% of retailers in North America are adopting RFID with a view to full adoption. After all, knowing the whereabouts of your product is key to being able to roll out an effective omnichannel offering. The majority of retailers worldwide adopt RFID for the technology's most well-known use case: inventory accuracy And of course, inventory visibility means less mark-downs and more selling at full price; coincidentally why a growing number of UK retailers are opting out of the annual discount orgy which is Black Friday (more of that post-Thanksgiving).

Then factor in that 30% of returns are returned to store and the case for RFID becomes clearer. But whilst inventory accuracy remains the number one reason and use case for adopting RFID, retailers are now beginning to unlock more reasons to adopt it. Since 2012, Burberry began implementing RFID within some of their flagship stores: We have started to initiate the use of RFID technology throughout our Burberry product lines to assist with stock and quality control, while also enhancing the customer experience in selected stores

Burberry

By using their smartphone to interact with RFID tags in store, Burberry shoppers can unlock extra content such as how that coat was made, the origins of those boots or which lipstick is right for their skin tone. Which is why in London last week, at TechStyle, Diebold-Nixdorf's fashion pop-up store of the future, RFID was the star turn. Showcasing many technologies, the 'store' demonstrated a more frictionless shopping experience just around the corner. No longer an expensive luxury, RFID is now key to unlocking omnichannel success.

The Retail Perfect Storm And Why Old Retail Is Broken Forever

First published in Forbes 29 November 2018

Traditional retail is under threat like never before. Rising costs, waning consumer confidence, online - all threatening the very viability of some retail businesses. And of course, here in the U.K. pantomime season is in full swing- aka Brexit. And there's another trend which is eroding the retail landscape; we see them everywhere - in city centres and shopping malls, where once it would have been a rarity if at all, today it has become the norm. And they are challenging the very definition of what it means to be a retailer, taking great chunks out of the retail pie. Sonos, Dyson, Casper to name a few are all doing it. Yes, manufacturers are rapidly realizing the benefits of going direct to the consumer.

These have all opened stores and now are joined by others, such as Away luggage. Apart from making great suitcases, they boast of selling direct to the consumer thus eliminating the traditional wholesale and retail mark-ups. Put with all the other pressures on retailers today and it's creating the perfect storm.

Back in the day

It wasn't always like this of course; back in the day long before the pesky internet, retailers could afford to be fairly sangfroid about life. Keep filling the shelves and the punters will come and buy stuff; not a problem. In those days, it seemed they couldn't get enough space, opening more and more stores for fun. Manufacturer, wholesaler, retailer - consumer. Everyone was happy.

Then some online bookstore called Amazon started up in the mid-nineties. Traditional (old) retail hardly gave the upstart a second look. Not only that, what was this new techie thing called the internet anyway? People would never buy from some faceless entity without feeling and touching the product. Why would anyone want to buy something online when they could go to a store instead? It is a sad truth that in the corridors of power in old retail, there inhabited many dinosaurs who thought that the internet represented just another passing trend which would quickly disappear leaving old retail to happily continue as it had done for decades. History would show that not only was this rather short-sighted, it set many on the path to ruin.

A new normal

Fast forward to 2018 and of course that short sightedness of old retail becomes very clear and obvious; well, to everyone except old retail it seems. Because old retail still clings to metrics which belong in the 80's; sales per employee, average transaction value and the most irrelevant of all: sales per square foot. Measuring anything and everything in the belief that this is the only way to run a retail business. But as we know, that model is no longer fit for purpose. New retail understands this. New retail understands that in order to survive, it has to care about things like, 'how is my customer feeling today?' or 'how can I deliver this to my customer wherever they might be?'

Because new retail doesn't carry the baggage of old retail it can do these things, ask itself these questions. It can change on a continual basis, it is not afraid to take risks, it realises that its customers always have a choice. Where old retail is organised around its own metrics, new retail is organised around the customer. Where old retail is set in its ways and believes that all it has to do is work harder to achieve success, new retail obsesses about constant change and innovation for the benefit of its customers. The perfect storm is creating an environment where the very essence of what it is to be a retailer is being redefined. New retail gets this, which is why the future is bright for new retail and decidedly bleak for old retail.

The Ghost Of Retail Yet To Come

First published in Forbes 13 December 2018

A Christmas Carol, that classic Dickens novel depicting the story of Ebenezer Scrooge and his miserly ways, transformed by a ghostly visit one Christmas Eve, endures to this day and is a cautionary tale for all of us. 'Tis the season to be jolly, joy to all and for retailers, 'tis the season to welcome that satisfying ringing of the tills. But so far, they must be feeling more like poor Bob Cratchit. "November trading was the worst on record, unbelievably bad...couldn't have predicted it...it will smash retailers to pieces." Pretty strong stuff.

And you'd be forgiven for thinking that this is the product of some sensationalist tabloid newspaper but you'd be wrong, for these are the words of Mike Ashley, the billionaire owner of Sports Direct Group, speaking during a trading update earlier today. It is hard to imagine a tougher time for retail; the perfect storm of rising costs, online competition, low consumer confidence compounded by Brexit uncertainty, are all taking their toll. The ghost of retail yet to come looms scarily large, its gnarled finger pointing to a deathly vision and, just like Scrooge, we should fear it, for the sense of foreboding is palpable.

Ghost of retail yet to come

But what of the future? According to GlobalData, "low consumer confidence and confusion over Brexit will inhibit big-ticket spend" this Christmas, traditionally the peak trading period in the 'golden quarter' - the last three months of the year. It's a pretty sobering thought that trading is unlikely to be anything other than disappointing, coming as it does, at the end of a year which has seen multiple store closures, CVA's and administrations. According to The Telegraph, amongst the major retailers, 1,267 shops have closed or been earmarked for closure during 2018, putting 25,159 jobs at risk.

And the Centre for Retail Research reports that amongst medium to large retail businesses, since 2007 a staggering 456 have failed, including 38 so far in 2018 alone (we've still got two weeks to go, anything could happen!) However, whilst the warnings have been there for some time, perhaps no-one could have predicted the extreme levels of uncertainty which Brexit has brought; wreaking havoc on the High Street in an unprecedented manner. For retail businesses, cash flow is everything, it is the very lifeblood of the business, without which it starves and ultimately perishes. And that is now under threat for many. But despite all the external influences at work, one can't help but wonder if, without them, would the picture actually be any different?

As we know, old retail is no longer fit for purpose and the changing of the guard is taking place right before our eyes. The ghost of retail yet to come casts a long dark shadow on the High Street, it's cold outside and there's a chill wind sweeping through the sector which shows no sign of abating. Scrooge managed to change his ways and was all the better for it. The question is, can retail? Whatever else happens, 2019 is likely to provide us with the answer.

M&S Turns To Investors To Buy Into Online Grocery Market

First published in Forbes 28 February 2019

"I would not go online if it was unprofitable to do so and would destroy shareholder value."

Steve Rowe, M&S Chief Executive

The news of the marriage this week between M&S and Ocado came as no surprise, embattled M&S chairman, Archie Norman, couldn't sit on his hands indefinitely, a stellar retail reputation was in danger of being tarnished and he had to do something. He needed to make a big play, and that's exactly what he did. What was more of a surprise however was that not only did he shell out a cool £750 million for a 50% stake in Ocado's retail business - not the underlying technology behind it - but that M&S shareholders will have to stump up £600 million to help pay for it *and* suffer a hefty cut in the dividend. It will take all of Archie Norman's conciliatory skills to placate a group of rather underwhelmed investors.

The joint venture will be called Ocado and will deliver M&S grocery products from September 2020 at the latest, when Ocado's deal with Waitrose expires. On Wednesday, M&S shares were down 8% while Ocado was up 4%; we knew who might be wearing a bigger smile. However, M&S chief executive, Steve Rowe was positive about the deal. 'We think we've paid a fair price' he said. "It's the only way we could have gone online within an immediately scalable, profitable and sustainable business", he added.

Mixed reaction

News of the deal met with mixed reactions, with an almost equal split between those who felt it was a good move for both parties and those who felt that first, it would be detrimental to consumers and that M&S had paid far too much for their stake in the joint venture. M&S have bought into the Ocado delivery service and not the underlying technology and while answers to the cause of the recent fire which gutted Ocado's Andover distribution centre are not yet forthcoming, it remains a question mark over the ultimate viability of the robotic technology heavily deployed by Ocado. For Ocado, the move makes perfect sense, meaning chief executive Tim Steiner is able to pursue his technology vision of supplying his automated, robotic solution to grocery businesses globally as opposed to being mired in the day to day operational issues of the retail business. For M&S it is not so clear, while it catapults them into the online grocery home delivery market, will the price ultimately prove too costly?

The big question is whether hitherto loyal Waitrose customers will be happy to switch to M&S, the choice for them is simple: They could choose to stay with Ocado and switch to buying M&S goods or they could switch to Waitrose.com which operates its own online delivery service. With the current contract with Ocado expiring in September 2020, Waitrose has been making moves to strengthen their own online delivery service and this might persuade many to remain loyal to a grocer they know and trust. Ultimately, however, it should be seen as a good move for M&S, according to figures from IGD, the online grocery delivery business in the U.K. is forecast to grow from £11.3bn to £17.2bn by 2023. Faced with that market growth, M&S simply couldn't afford to sit and watch any longer.

New PwC Survey Reveals Consumer Data Is The Most Highly Valued

First published in Forbes 4 March 2019

The results of a survey conducted by PwC published today suggest that data will be the most important consideration in 2019 and that consumer data is the most valuable for companies to harvest. And in PwC's 22nd Annual Global CEO survey, 94% consider data on customer and client preferences/needs as critical or important. It's been accepted that for some time, data is the key to unlocking customer value and when it comes to predicting trends in retail, in 2019 data, or more importantly, the smart use of customer data is now firmly at the top of the list. According to the survey - of nearly 300 CEOs in the U.S. in companies with a turnover in excess of $500 million - 86% of businesses say 2019 is the year in which they will race to extract value from data. And perhaps what is more revealing is that 88% say that in 2019 they have the potential to pull ahead of their rivals in this race.

According to PwC, "Customer data that feeds new value propositions, new and improved experiences, and new revenue models is how winners will distance themselves from the pack". But of course, the challenge as always is how we can trust the quality and integrity of the data. This is a huge challenge. According to PwC, the solution is *trusted data optimization*: an approach that enhances organizational trust in data and its uses while enabling rapid, risk-based decisions about how to turn data into value.

The data most businesses want

Top of the list for companies wishing to extract value from data is consumer data, PwC's Pulse Survey reveals. Further, it shows that executives particularly value data on consumer preferences, current and predicted. Data, of course, can, for example, enable retailers to target promotions and products to individual consumers. That much we've known but now for the first time, many executives are realizing that data and artificial intelligence (AI) can provide the key to unlocking a whole new era of consumer engagement. As if to underline the value of data, according to research at the University of Texas, two billion dollars annually would be the average revenue boost to Fortune 1000 companies from increasing data's usability by just 10%. There are, of course, obstacles to maximizing the usability of data such as regulatory and fears over the inaccuracy of the data both currently held and yet to gather.

But those will be overcome and when they are, we can expect a new age of personalisation the likes of which we've only imagined until now. The question remains, however, will we be ready to accept it?

Iceland Foods – More Than You Think

First published in Forbes 12 March 2019

"We need to leave a light footprint on the planet....it's about consumerism, not absolute population"

Richard Walker, Iceland MD

Back in January, I wrote a piece on Iceland entitled 'Why trust should always be the beating heart of retail', and went on to share my views on the supermarket chain's claims regarding the use of and subsequent removal of palm oil from their own label products. This, by all accounts, did not go down too well in the corridors of Deeside (home to Iceland Foods) and so it was that I met in London recently with Iceland MD Richard Walker and Iceland's Director of Corporate Affairs, Keith Hann, there ostensibly to talk all things palm oil. But, as it transpired, in an illuminating conversation, we discussed a great deal more than just palm oil, and it soon became apparent that what motivates Iceland's boss is a deep and sincere passion for the environment and for doing the right thing for the planet.

Retail, being so visible, has a responsibility to do far more than it currently does for the environment, he asserts, and that while Iceland is in business to 'do well and make a profit' this must be balanced against its social responsibility. He describes himself as an 'agitator' and of being pleased that the business 'punches above its weight'. But there's more to it than that.

On the palm oil campaign, he is clearly proud of the fact that it has raised public awareness of the issue and is at pains to stress that he is not anti-palm oil, but that it is the deforestation and destruction of the natural habitat of the wildlife of Malaysia and Indonesia - most notably orangutans - that he is so against. And on that subject, there is a potential breakthrough as the world's largest palm oil producer, Wilmar, has said that it is stepping up its efforts to produce palm oil with zero deforestation. Creating the debate and effecting change was, says Richard, the primary aim of the campaign and in that respect, he would appear to have been successful.

Protecting the planet

Palm oil, however, is but one of many subjects which he is passionate about. Industrialized fishing being another where he says, 'in our oceans, it's completely lawless' and as we discuss the vital role our oceans play in the survival of the planet, the subject inevitably turns to the use of plastics and the harm they cause to marine life.

Iceland has committed to eliminating the use of plastics in its own label products by 2023. And as Richard points out, there is no such thing as plastic recycling, the best that can be achieved is 'downcycling' thus the priority must be on the use of alternative materials or none at all. As a challenge, the elimination of palm oil looks like a walk in the park when compared to eliminating plastics, our dependence and the complexity of the supply chain meaning a far greater horizon for achieving the goal. However, he points to some quick wins, such as the replacement of black plastic ready meal trays with FSC certified board trays.

Another trial is taking place in Liverpool at one of Iceland's Food Warehouse stores, where a step back to traditional greengrocers is resulting in loose fruit and veg. This is currently under review as it requires a fundamental shift in shopping behaviour but Richard is keen to try these different options for merchandising, provided they help with the overall objective of reducing the amount of plastic, as he points out, 'every minute there's a truckload of plastic which enters the oceans'.

And for those retail businesses who are not, perhaps, as forthright and bold with their environmental initiatives, it is worth remembering that in the main it is the consumers of tomorrow - generation Z - who most wish to associate themselves with a brand which is environmentally friendly. Retail is more than simply generating profit, retail has a social responsibility and perhaps the third fastest growing supermarket might just provide the template for that.

PART SEVEN: PHOENIX

When I set out to write this book, I quickly realised that what commands the headlines these days is mostly negative. Retail is closest to all of us and is the most relevant sector as it touches our lives like no other. Hence it is always making the news and usually when there are store closures, staff redundancies, administrations and so forth. But that is only one part of the picture and is a consequence of the huge upheaval and transformation which retail is currently experiencing. Indeed, the very nature and definition of what it means to be a retailer, is rapidly being re-written. But the underlying message for me is that what we are witnessing is not the death of the high street but the rebirth. And that is something to be celebrated not mourned.

Which is why this, the final part, is named 'Phoenix'. These are incredibly tough times for retail but they are also incredibly exciting times and we have many reasons to feel optimistic about the future. New retail will rise stronger and more inspiring than ever before and with it, retail will find a new, more relevant and more exciting place in all our lives. It may look a little different from today's incarnation, but I'm sure, will be the better for it. And when can we expect to see this 'new retail' I hear you ask? That depends on many factors. Today, especially in the fashion sector, there are many bright young things who are challenging the status quo like never before. I for one look forward to the day when they are in positions of influence or even running retail businesses because it is then that we should expect to see the transformation accelerate still further.

But in order to fulfil its potential, retail needs a little help. Watching the 2018 budget delivered by Philip Hammond, it struck me a) how little the government understands the nature of the challenges facing retail and b) that they somehow believe it to be a retail problem, for retail to solve. This of course, couldn't be further from the truth. I've touched on business rates elsewhere in this book and so won't cover the same ground again suffice to say that the very first step that central government needs to take is to reform the entire system of business rates. The same £30 billion can be recouped by the Treasury but in a far fairer and more equitable fashion. Creating this level playing field will then allow everyone to compete on equal terms. The good will still be good and the underperforming will at least have the chance to compete in a fairer manner.

Lest we forget, retail is the beating heart of all our communities because the high street has traditionally relied on retail for its growth and survival. Some may say that it has relied far too much on retail and it is this transformation that we are now witnessing. The birth of the 'new high street' is both an exciting and intoxicating prospect for it most certainly will have a broader variety of shops, restaurants, bars, gyms, social centres, residential space and so on. Retail and the high street are not dying, they just need a little help.

eBay's Emotion Store Gives A Glimpse Into The Future

First published in Retail Week 6 December 2016

Imagine a world where a smile or a frown dictates what food is presented to you, or one where your mood determines which clothes you buy. A world where your emotions decide the contents of your shopping basket sounds far-fetched. Somewhat Orwellian.

Well, thanks to eBay, I was able to enter this world via its "emotionally powered" pop-up store in London last week. The store, which was open for just 48 hours, was created in partnership with California-based emotion tech start-up company Lightwave, and used bio-analytic technology to determine which products consumers truly like. To experience this, I was allocated a booth where, using noise-cancelling headphones and an interactive screen, I browsed various products, ranging from a Dyson vacuum cleaner to a Christmas-themed onesie. Using facial coding and biometric sensors incorporated into each booth, my emotional reaction to each product was recorded by detecting over 100,000 tiny facial movements.

The results of which were then captured both on a huge 'emotional tapestry' screen and in an individual report emailed to me (apparently, I loved the Dyson). Billed as the 'ultimate do good, feel good' shop, set within the context of giving at Christmas, it could be said to be a little gimmicky, but that would miss the point.

"On the basis of this, retailers could present a truly personalised experience" Lightwave chief executive Rana June told me that this was its first foray into retail, having previously proved the technology in such arenas as the US presidential race, detecting voters' emotional responses to a Hillary Clinton speech, or in the NFL by monitoring the fans' reactions to the play. Now imagine a world where, whether it be online or in-store, the retailer is able to detect your likes and dislikes from not only your browsing behaviour but from what sort of mood you are in. On the basis of this, retailers could present a truly personalised experience.

For me, this was a great demonstration of the potential of technology to rapidly revolutionise our shopping experience, and that is to be applauded. Whether stores of the future will have 'emotion walls' remains to be seen, but one thing's for sure – it's all a far cry from nappies and beer.

A Fabulously British Affair At Jack Wills

First published in Retail Reflections 20 December 2016

Take one medieval market town in Surrey, add a Grade II-listed 17th-century manor house where Sir Winston Churchill once stayed, then introduce an iconic British retail brand. What do you get? A unique in-store experience like no other. For behind the magnificent Georgian façade of this Jack Wills outlet in Reigate lies a real gem.

The house, over its three floors, is arranged just as it would have been. Founded in Salcombe 17 years ago by Robert Shaw and chief executive Peter Williams, Jack Wills has become the archetypal British brand – the sign outside proclaiming 'outfitters to the gentry' – carving a special niche amongst the well-heeled university generation. Much is written about technology driving in-store experience, but this espouses none of that. The sheer majesty of the house – for it really shouldn't be described as a store – is such that there really is no need for technology. On entering, the grand hallway is all wood panelling and bare floorboards, lending a marvellous patina to the experience. But this is no show home – its age very clear – and it is all the better for it. It is as if you have been invited round to a warm, convivial house party. I'm told the house, over its three floors, is arranged just as it would have been.

The magnificent hallway has a staircase leading enticingly to further rooms upstairs whilst the large drawing room leading off the hallway is filled with merchandise laid out using some of the original fixtures and fittings. On chatting to the store colleagues, it is clear that they love the place and recognise how special the house - as they refer to it - is. Floorboards creak underfoot as I make my way upstairs, however nothing could have prepared me for what I was about to encounter. As the faded sign on the wall indicates, I am about to enter the 'bathing room'. Sash windows, wooden shutters, or recessed window seats I might have expected. But right in the centre of the room, filled with Jack Wills merchandise, is an old roll-top bath. Could this be where Sir Winston once had a soak? Even the old loo is still in situ.

Exploring further to the top floor, I encounter the fitting rooms which are laid out as a bedroom. Simply stunning. This is in-store experience on steroids. We often refer to the theatre of retail and there are some great examples (think Liberty, Selfridges, Fortnum & Mason). But little comes close to this. If you're seeking inspiration and an antidote to the unrelenting march of technology, this might just be for you.

The Times They Are A-Changin'

First published in Retail Reflections 17 July 2017

Bob Dylan couldn't have put it better when he wrote those lyrics back in 1964. And the times certainly are changing if you're an internet or retail marketer; a change so profound that the entire way in which you engage with your audience is shifting beyond all recognition.

Content is king and why context is queen bee!

Here's a great quote from fellow IBM Futurist, Martin Jones: "Social is how customers hear about you, search is how they find you BUT content is how they'll remember you". And that's not all, according to London based consultancy Olapic, 76% of consumers view content posted by other consumers as more honest than advertising. As consumers, we are seeking ever more personalised brand experiences. We want brands to engage with us, not broadcast to us.

Data: the new oil

Not only that, new data is being created on an unprecedented scale. You might be familiar with data being measured in gigabytes – such as the amount of gigabytes of space left on your smartphone and how you're always running out. According to Citrix, by the end of 2016 there was more than a zettabyte of data in the world. To put that in context, to view 1 zettabyte of data in HD video would take you 152 million years. And by 2020 it is estimated that there will be 44 zettabytes of data in the world. And much of this is being created by consumers, not brands.

Consumers know brands better than they do themselves and they want a slice of it. We want to influence and shape the world around us like never before. Each and every day, we are putting out our digital footprint or signature for anyone to capture. And we expect brands to be doing so. This is why Content is King but Context is Queen Bee. Content needs to engage, excite, inspire but if it's not in the right place at the right time and targeted in the right way it is wasted. Personalised, targeted content is now the most critical element of a brands' marketing campaign.

In the same research from Olapic: "86% of young millennials (aged 18-24) share brand photos to express product appreciation with friends"

Today's consumer journey

There was a time when marketers could plot the consumer journey with reasonable accuracy; not any more. What once was awareness, consideration & then purchase is now a jumbled minefield much akin to 3D snakes and ladders where we shift, backtrack, change channels, seek positive peer reviews, research in many different ways. This is leading brands to realise the value of content in its many forms whether it be text, video or images.

We want to have our lives enriched and immerse ourselves in a brand and its products in ways never before imagined. And that's not all, we want to feel we have the ability to influence those brands with our feedback and comments. Timberland is a great example of a brand which realises this and seeks to engage its customers with great content. Through partnerships, influencers and celebrities they seek to 'amplify & enable the lifestyle".

Thirty Million Bubbles

First published in Retail Reflections 14 October 2017

What do you get if you take one amazing brewery experience, a great agenda and then add an audience packed with some of the best retail minds in Ireland? Retail Ireland Summit 2017 of course! Organised by Retail Ireland and Ibec the topic for discussion this year was 'Exploring Experiential Retail' – something which clearly resonated as witnessed by a packed room for this year's conference. And so it was that I found myself in Dublin at 'The Home of Guinness' otherwise known as the Guinness Storehouse this week, there at the invitation of Retail Ireland and Ibec.

And what an apt venue to choose to discuss experiential retail. The Guinness Storehouse attracts 1.6 million visitors a year from all around the world and is Ireland's top tourist attraction. No wonder for it has grown into an iconic destination, and a 'must see' for everyone when in Dublin. Retail Ireland is tireless in its efforts to help and support the Irish retail sector and how it can future proof itself against the rapidly changing retail environment. As a forerunner to the conference, earlier this year it published 'Shaping the Future of Irish Retail 2020' a new and ambitious strategy for the sector.

Founded on four key pillars – Competitiveness, Confidence, Careers and Community – it is a blueprint for the Irish retail sector and the conference took its cues from that. Clearly, from what we heard, the Irish economy is in rude health however the challenges facing retail are both sustained and enduring.

Inspiring retail

In my role as a retail analyst and IBM Futurist, I get to attend a lot of retail conferences and seminars. Never before has the subject of customer experience and the consumer featured so strongly. Faced with the stiffest competition ever seen, retailers are having to reinvent themselves and in particular this means their literal shop window - their stores – are having to completely rethink their role and the value that they can offer. No longer simply a place to visit to purchase goods off the shelf, stores must now become enjoyable destinations where we wish to spend time. But make no mistake, the reward for getting it right is there to be had – engage, inspire and connect. In the same week as Sears announced that it was shuttering all of its stores in Canada with the loss of 12,000 jobs, the Retail Ireland Summit provided plenty of insights into how retailers can attract and retain customers.

Whether it means being smart with the investment in technology, embracing storytelling, understanding the value of data when it comes to delivering true personalisation or becoming a customer centric organisation from the inside out, there was plenty to digest and takeaway in terms of valuable practical advice for any retailer looking at the next stage of growth and development. And what of all those bubbles? After the conference we made our way to the Gravity Bar at the top of the Guinness Storehouse to savour a pint of the black stuff - each containing 30 million bubbles. A great end to a great day.

Everyone's Welcome

First published in Retail Reflections 1 December 2017

The date is 22nd September 2014 – one that will go down in history as one of the darkest in UK retail history. The headlines were damning, for it was on this day that it emerged that new Tesco Chief Executive Dave Lewis had advised the City that Tesco profits had been overstated by £250m. Four executives were suspended and £2bn was wiped off the share value. It represented a nadir for the once high flying, now beleaguered grocer.

The great British public can be fickle at the best of times and during those dark days we relished in giving that bastion of the UK High Street a right royal kicking. From the way it treated suppliers to the corporate arrogance stalking the corridors of Welwyn - suddenly everything the brand stood for was under attack. Whilst we might have fallen out of love with the brand; we also wanted to make a point. Fast forward to late November 2017 and I am with Tesco Chief Customer Officer, Alessandra Bellini and Group Communications Director, Jane Lawrie at the offices of their creative agency BBH, there to discuss the business and to preview the 2017 Tesco Christmas ad campaign.

Reason to believe

I am warmly thanked for coming; the atmosphere is convivial and friendly. We discuss the past and it is clear that lessons have been learnt - but what comes across as most striking of all is the sheer humility of it all. The Tesco reluctance to engage is legendary but all that appears to have gone, the new management team under Dave Lewis singing from a very different hymn sheet. The conversation is peppered with words like 'emotional engagement' and 'real people, real stories' and 'we need to earn the trust of our customers'.

Encouragingly, this is translating into a much brighter performance; the interim results announced in October showing a sharp rise in first half profits to £562m together with the resumption of dividend payments. And all this has been achieved in the face of fierce competition from the discounters – not an easy trick to pull off. Which leaves me reflecting on the new Tesco we are witnessing rather than the previous bloated incarnation. In some way or other the High Street needs a Tesco – in reality, the great British public needs a Tesco - and on the evidence of this, we're well on the way to falling back in love with a brand that, if truth be known, just needed to be put in its place.

New Thinking Needed For Healthy High Streets

First published in Retail Week 6 March 2018

You don't need me to tell you that the outlook for 2018 remains pretty grim with many retailers struggling to keep their heads above water. The twin forces of Brexit and inflation are combining to create uncertainty and a loss of consumer confidence. A look at the GfK UK consumer confidence index is revealing; stubbornly negative for the past 12 months and despite a slight blip in January 2018, there appears no sign of lasting recovery.

In the face of this however, our expectations as consumers continue to grow, fuelled by a seemingly insatiable thirst for immediate gratification and 'anything anywhere'. Next day delivery, same day delivery, jeans for a tenner, strawberries in January, click-and-collect, deliver to me… the list goes on. But are we sleepwalking into the abyss? Are our expectations of retailers getting out of hand? Should we be educated to expect less so that our favourite brands can at least make a decent margin and continue to stay in business? The evidence points to the contrary.

For example, according to a study conducted by American Express and Forrester, Gen Z (those born post-1995) are more than twice as likely than millennials to drop a brand for poor features or responsiveness on social media.
This increasing demand being placed on retailers by all demographics is stretching their capability to the point of breaking.

Social implications

Talk of a retail apocalypse is great for grabbing the headlines, however the shift in attitudes and behaviour has significant implications not just for retail but for society as a whole. Here's why. Up and down the country, whichever town or city you care to think of, the centre of that community is the high street. It is a meeting place, a social centre – somewhere to not only to shop, but to dine out, meet people, be entertained. The high street is the heartbeat of every community up and down the country. But are we systematically destroying it with our unrealistic expectations? There seems no end in sight. The genie is out of the bottle and it would be a brave person who tried to put it back. It's become a question of who blinks first and of course no one is about to do that – literally prepared to go out of business rather than break ranks, desperately trying to keep up with the latest service and delivery innovations.

Elevating the discussion

Rather than headline grabbing, the discussion must be elevated for it involves many bodies not directly in the retail industry; the government, councils, planners, etc, all that have a part to play.

There have been attempts of course to put this on the agenda, most notably the Mary Portas 'save the high street' campaign and the Grimsey Review, a report into what can be done to reinvigorate Britain's town centres. But a combination of short sightedness, political agendas and apathy on the part of the stakeholders involved stymied both. In the case of the former, the 12 towns featured have between them lost nearly a net 1,000 shops in the period since 2012. This decline is echoed by data from Retail Futures, which reported that in the six years between 2012 and 2018 some 22 per cent of shops will have closed.

Who knows where we are heading but one thing is for sure — if we are to remain a nation of shopkeepers, the issue cannot be ignored. As they say, be careful what you wish for.

Jack's: Back To The Future?

First published in Retail Reflections 20 September 2018

Remember the date: 20th September 2018. Because this is the date when Tesco launched their new discount brand Jack's onto the UK High Street. At the press conference held at the Chatteris Jack's store the day before, there was a positive media scrum. Over 100 crammed in to hear what Tesco CEO Dave Lewis had to tell us about the fascia designed to take on rivals Aldi and Lidl head on. Part of the Tesco family but otherwise not (no online and no club card points), Jack's is a curious mix: one analyst describing it as being 'the biggest compliment to Aldi and Lidl' whilst most felt it had been executed well.

Such was the magnitude of the occasion that even Dave Lewis was hard pressed to remember when Tesco last launched a new brand. So, what conclusions can we make so far? The concept appears well thought through; relying heavily on the heritage of Tesco, we were treated to a video montage highlighting the milestones in their journey from Tesco Tea and the first store in Burnt Oak opened in 1929 to founder Jack Cohen's epiphany in 1946 when he saw the self-service supermarkets in the US to the present day and the 'loss of sight of the customer' in more recent times. But this left this writer wondering how many of the good folk of Chatteris had ever heard of Jack Cohen, much less care? The key here can perhaps be taken from what UK CEO Jason Tarry had to say: "We wanted to get back to being the champion of the customer". Carrying just 2,600 lines - 1,800 of which are Jack's own brand the stores are a much simpler version of Tesco and play strongly to being British; indeed, this mantra was repeated over and over by anyone present who was wearing a Tesco badge - 8 out of 10 products stocked are British.

In the words of their inspiration, Jack Cohen, Jack's are designed to be 'no fuss, no frills, simple and warm'. Tapping into the Brexit fervour sweeping the country? But currently the plans show that they don't appear to want to be the cheapest in many towns. Two stores - Chatteris in Cambridgeshire and Immingham in Lincolnshire have opened today with plans for just 10 to 15 to follow. Repurposing space (Chatteris was originally due to be a Tesco Extra but was mothballed in 2014) forms a focal part of the strategy.

"Our intention is to be the cheapest in town" Dave Lewis, Tesco CEO. This begs the question: is this an elaborate centenary celebration or a trojan horse for a much bigger entry into the discount market. In the words of one analyst I spoke to at the press launch "this seems to be more of a property exercise than anything else". Time will tell but for now the good people of Chatteris have just got themselves a great new addition to their supermarket experience.

Artificial Intelligence: Saint Or Sinner?

First published in Forbes 7 December 2018

Here's a question for the digital age: in a car crash involving an autonomous vehicle and a pedestrian, who dies? The pedestrian or the passengers? Well, let's hope neither because I for one wouldn't wish to be faced with that conundrum but it needs answering before we witness widespread adoption of autonomous vehicles. Neither are we about to see our skies filled with drones, frantically crisscrossing the skies making deliveries up and down the country. Since July this year, in the U.K. it has been illegal to fly a drone above 120 meters, pilots require a license from the Civil Aviation Authority and there are strict guidelines for usage.

A little closer to home, although not life-threatening, many businesses are faced with the dilemma of whether to declare their call centre chatbots as being just that or whether to let the caller make assumptions as to the provenance of the 'person' on the other end of the phone. Online grocer Ocado plans to use digital assistants in the next 12 months but this will be to supplement call centre chat, "Artificial Intelligence (AI) can't resolve complex issues, that needs human interaction" according to Head of Operations Ian Pattle when speaking at a recent event in London. You might, therefore, be forgiven for thinking that the future's a bit bleak for AI, after all, we don't want artificial, we want artisan and authentic. Don't we?

Saint or sinner?

Assisted Intelligence, Augmented Intelligence - we all have our favourites and they don't usually include 'artificial'. IBM is perhaps most well-known for Watson and it was once put to me to think of Watson as like having 'hundreds of little Einstein's running around at your every beck and call'. And whilst AI is becoming more and more ubiquitous - Spotify and Netflix being two examples of personalization being driven on virtually a one to one basis meanwhile Huawei claim that AI resides in my new P20 Pro smartphone to ensure crystal clear pictures even in very low light (it works) - I have a feeling that we are yet to experience the great AI epiphany.

Hyper-personalization is an area ripe for massive development and AI provides the means to achieve this. Retailers are notoriously reluctant to disclose details of their use of AI (which in most cases is still in its relative infancy) and perhaps this is the clearest sign we have that they also realize the huge potential of AI. One who has bucked this trend, however, is U.K. streetwear and sportswear retailer, Footasylum PLC which claims to have seen a 28 percent increase in email revenue from hyper-personalized marketing communications using AI as the engine to drive this. "Customers now expect high levels of personalization at every single touchpoint."- Tom Makin, e-commerce and marketing director at Footasylum. Delivering a highly relevant experience to each and every one of their customers is clearly paying dividends and this is why AI is so critical to the success of retail brands, whether online or in-store.

More than ever we expect a personalized experience and when we don't get it, we simply move on to the next brand who are able to deliver against our expectations. And for those who do, the rewards in terms of greater customer loyalty and growth are bearing fruit. We may not have experienced the AI epiphany in retail just yet, however, we soon will; and when we do, retail will be changed forever.

Best Of Times, Worst Of Times: What Does 2019 Have In Store For Retail?

First published in Forbes 31 December 2018

'Tis the season to be, well, frankly a bit optimistic for once? If 2018 was challenging is the New Year likely to serve up anything different? As we collectively recover from the turkey and Christmas pudding and find ourselves in that traditional period of limbo between Christmas and the New Year, here's a look ahead to the year nearly upon us.

Rising costs, low consumer confidence, Brexit tearing the country apart, the dying High Street, online competition and the weather. Yes, like that Christmas turkey, we've all probably had enough of it by now. Spoiler alert: expect to continue to hear plenty more about the 'retail apocalypse' as we enter the New Year, but let's take a moment and consider what's really happening out there.

The real state of the nation

OK, so let's get real; we're not about to stop eating or putting clothes on our backs or buying that latest smartphone. No, of course, we're not about to stop 'consuming' but two things are very apparent; the volume and nature of our consumption are changing. Rapidly and irreversibly. Less discretionary, focusing more on the need. This will continue into 2019 and as concerns over Brexit become more and more acute this behaviour will only be exacerbated.

Brexit or no Brexit, not just the first quarter of the year, but the first half of the year is going to be extremely tough. Couple this uncertainty with a different kind of consumption, one characterized increasingly by a mobile commerce (many would say ruinous) returns epidemic sweeping through retail, and the challenge that most are facing suddenly appears almost insurmountable. Some forty trading updates from U.K. retailers are expected in January; it's not going to be pretty. Sadly, HMV has already announced its second administration in six years. For the majority at best - survival. At worst - administration. Let's hope that the former state prevails. Should we be concerned by all this?

The short answer is yes, because we need a healthy retail sector. That's worth repeating because many appear oblivious to it. We need a healthy retail sector. And that's not simply because of the three million-plus people which it employs but because it is the beating heart of our towns and cities. Retail and the High Street need to survive for the good of our communities.

What to expect in 2019

Well, for a start, what not to expect: thousands of drones filling our skies. Even without the recent Gatwick Airport farce, (drones are now officially a 'bad thing') drone deliveries are still years away (will be interesting to revisit this one in twelve months' time). Add to that, autonomous vehicles; why? Because the fundamental, moral and possibly unanswerable question of who dies in an accident has yet to be resolved. Granny? The two young children? Mother? Father? It's too horrible to contemplate.

However, one thing is for sure, in a never-ending search to quench our thirst for anytime, anywhere delivery, more and more automation will be deployed. Delivery within the hour to wherever we are will become the expected norm by the end of 2019. Coupled with dynamic delivery there will be hyper-personalization which will make today's version seem crude, to say the least. I for one am looking forward to the time when my favourite brands predict my needs and wants and begin to add real value to my life. The age of consumer pull, as opposed to brand push, is virtually upon us. And yes, you read the last two sentences correctly; they're not contradictory. My digital self will ensure that what appears to be a push is actually a response to my online pull. Exciting times.

Our love affair with online has shown no sign of abating in 2018; over the next twelve months, however, we will begin to witness a slowdown in online growth as retailers finally bite the returns bullet and in-store comes back into fashion. And if the volume of returns is down to inconsistent sizing, then we will start to see more and more technology solutions creating accurate sizing measurements which will reduce the number of returns. Good news for everyone. However, whether we will begin to see the green shoots of a level playing field in 2019 is still open to question. Virtually everyone except Government recognizes that the current system of taxation for retail businesses is outdated and no longer fit for purpose.

There are some signs that those in office are finally waking up to this but whether this leads to action is open to question. Let's hope good sense prevails. As we enter 2019, the popular dialogue would have us all believe that the High Street is practically dead already. Nothing could be further from the truth. But what is true is that we are in the midst of witnessing a changing of the guard. Old retail is making way for new retail and whilst there will be casualties along the way, as with any culling, it is for the greater good. And for that reason alone, we should remain optimistic about the prospects for retail in 2019.

High Velocity Retail: Why The World Retail Congress Was A Breath Of Fresh Air

First published in Forbes 16 May 2019

The World Retail Congress took place in Amsterdam this week. Nothing to shout about you might think, until you understand what was discussed at the conference. For this was no ordinary conference. Gone were the usual corporate presentations and platitudes, gone were the, frankly, dull sessions, rehashing the same old message we've heard at far too many retail conferences around the globe. Re-imaging retail, re-inventing retail blah blah blah. I was beginning to think that this was the staple diet which I was destined to have to consume for eternity. Not a bit of it. From the first to the last, it was nothing short of energising. Why? Because here was a conference not afraid to call out retail. To call out retail for not doing enough. To call out retail for sitting on its laurels, for not changing rapidly enough. For using too much plastic. For paying lip service to environmental issues. It was relentless.

Sustainability, however you might define it, was at the heart of many of the debates. And it is here that retail has to stand up and be counted. Speaker after speaker, gently or, in the case of Guy Singh Martin from Riverford, full on smashing you in the face, called out the industry and challenged it in ways this writer has not heard for a long time. But if all this sounds a little depressing, it certainly wasn't. On the contrary. Responsible retail and having a responsibility for being not only good corporate citizens but understanding its social responsibilities ran through the conference. I asked Steve Laughlin, Vice President and General Manager Consumer Industry for IBM and primary sponsor of the event for his thoughts and his words echoed that of the conference theme. "We're here not just to network and generate business but to be good (retail) corporate citizens and to support the industry".

And of course, as we know, the industry is faced with some massive challenges and is having to look at itself like never before. Almost philosophically, retail is having to ask itself the very essence of what it stands for. What value does it bring in a world more than ever populated by the direct to consumer model from brands such as Dyson, Nike, Adidas to name a few. No more is it acceptable or appropriate to simply sell stock. And in this regard, again, the conference surpassed expectations by going beyond the oft and overused term 'experiential' retail and offered up a vision of a future for retail where the very boundaries of what it means to be in retail, to be a retailer, become blurred and at the same time expanded.

The themes for the conference were 'high velocity retail' and 'the future of retail'. Both were both appropriate and in abundance for an industry which never fails to be out of the headlines, usually where there's yet another story of store closures, administrations, job losses and so forth. But whilst the challenge has never been greater, the industry has never been greater.

Lord Stuart Rose summed it up rather well: "The death of the high street is overblown. For the first time, retailers and landlords now realise that they need to work together. Retailers are in a unique place to build relationships of trust". And if the challenge to corporate social responsibility came through loud and clear, so did the human element of retail. Perhaps no other industry relies on human interaction, human engagement and human passions as much as retail. World Retail Congress - challenging retail to be the best that it can be. Long may it continue to be that way.

Why A Few Less Boots On The High Street Can Only Be Healthy

First published in Forbes 30 May 2019

In common with many young teenagers, when I was growing up, I didn't always appreciate being told what to do. Whether it be by my parents or my teachers, the urge to rebel was sometimes overwhelming. Tell me to do one thing and I'd do the polar opposite. Naturally, as the years go by, one progresses from spotty pubescence to young adulthood and (as in my case) to middle age. But that desire to rebel, just ever so slightly, still lingers in the deep recesses, ready to surface given the right conditions. And those conditions appear to come together every time I walk into a branch of the nation's favourite chemist - Boots. Which of course is hard to avoid because it seems every other shop on the high street is a branch of Boots. Or Boots the chemist. Or Boots the optician.

Like some sagely and overly pompous relative, presiding over all around them at the annual family gathering, lying in wait, ready to admonish the loud or the over-excited and tell them what's best for them. Never short of an unwanted word or two of advice, making us feel somehow inadequate and asking for permission where none is required. The epitome of the legacy retailer parent-child relationship with their customers which used to prevail up and down the high street, even to the extent of the white coats. One has to ask, is there a place for it any longer? After all, we can get our medicines online now. We can access a pharmacist online now. We can order anything we like online now (save for a haircut or the odd filling or two). So why do legacy retailers still survive when the younger, fitter, stronger, more agile players are chomping at the bit, waiting to take their place?

The answer: nostalgia. Our parents shopped at Boots and their parents before them. We are simply following in a long line of tradition. Need more ointment? Run out of nappy cream? Feeling poorly? No problem I'll just pop down to Boots the chemist. Are there any high streets, train stations or airports without one? After all, we can never have enough suncream, paracetamol or handcream can we? And then there are our prescriptions. Wouldn't trust them with anyone else, a Boots pharmacist knows what's best for us. Wouldn't go anywhere else. But just like that all-knowing relative, the world is rapidly changing around them without them seeming to realize. Still clinging to an outdated conversation while the family grows old around them. There is a good reason why we prune our rose bushes at this time of year. Without doing so they become weak and poorly shaped. Which is why fewer Boots on our high streets can only be a good thing.

From Opening His Own Bookstore To Running Barnes & Noble, The Incredible Journey Of James Daunt

First published in Forbes 8 June 2019

Pay attention, for I have a brief history lesson for you. It's the story of two, well three, actually, book stores, all selling books in different ways and how each survives to this day. The first, Barnes & Noble, can be traced right back to 1873, when Charles M. Barnes started a book business from his home in Wheaton, Illinois. In 1917, his son, William, went to New York to join G. Clifford Noble in establishing Barnes & Noble. Today Barnes & Noble is a Fortune 1000 company and has over 600 stores across the U.S.

In 1982, Tim Waterstone founded Waterstones book stores with £6,000 redundancy money. Waterstones was variously owned by WH Smith and HMV before the latter sold the business in 2011 to Alexander Mamut, the Russian billionaire, for just £53 million as it struggled itself for survival. Waterstones, now Britain's largest bookshop chain with 296 stores, was in need of investment and revitalizing and the new owner installed James Daunt at the helm and he set about transforming the business. By 2018 pre-tax profits had jumped 80% to £18 million. This valued the business at £200 million. And then in June 2018, Waterstones was acquired by hedge fund Elliott Advisers.

But we're getting ahead of ourselves. For it was in 1990 that James Daunt founded Daunt Books in London. Today there are six Daunt Books across the capital. And to bring our story up to date, the news this week that the struggling Barnes & Noble has been acquired by the owners of Waterstones, Elliott Advisers for $683 million - and appointed that same James Daunt as Chief Executive. The deal meaning that Daunt will continue as Chief Executive at Waterstones while spending time in New York turning around the ailing Barnes & Noble. From the opening of that bookstore at number 83 Marylebone High Street, on the site originally built for antiquarian booksellers Francis Edwards in 1910, it's been quite a journey for James Daunt.

Barnes & Noble has been listed on the New York stock exchange since 1993, but the chain suffered when Amazon entered the market in 1995, and the seeds of Barnes & Noble's decline were sowed. In 2014, Barnes & Noble closed its New York Fifth Avenue store - once the world's largest bookstore - and has faced declining sales over recent years. Last year it made a loss of $137.7m before tax on sales of $3.6bn. Meanwhile, under Daunts stewardship, the fortunes of Waterstones were going in the opposite direction.

Of course, Waterstones faced its own challenge from Amazon, but it returned to profit in 2016 after six years of losses. The key to this turnaround? Daunt oversaw a big investment in the stores, concentrating on turning them into places to browse and organizing more in-store events. Leonardo Riggio, chairman of Barnes & Noble, said: "We are pleased to have reached this agreement with Elliott, the owner of Waterstones, a bookseller I have admired over the years". More than anything, this is a story of how transforming the store experience can transform the fortunes of a retail business. Never a day seems to go by without reading more about 'in-store experience' and 'experiential' retail. And this is the story of how one man with a passion for books, believed that books should be enjoyed and not consigned to simply being sold online.

It is also a lesson that many would do well to learn from: that stores need constant maintenance and refreshing, for they are the very embodiment of the brand and must constantly give people a reason for crossing the threshold. It is also a very human story and for that reason, one to be celebrated. And all this is good news for Barnes & Noble who can, I'm sure, feel optimistic about the future.

AFTERWORD

During the time of writing and compiling this book, the list of well-known retailers and brands which have either closed stores, applied for a Company Voluntary Arrangement (CVA) or gone into administration is a who's who of the UK high street. Marks and Spencer, Debenhams, House of Fraser, Jamie's Italian, Boots, LK Bennett, and New Look to name a few.

To which the name of Arcadia can be added to the list. Not least because of the high profile of its owner, Sir Philip Green, Arcadia, at the time of writing, is grabbing its fair share of the headlines. Owing to the complex nature of the business, not one but seven CVAs have been filed. And the landlords don't like it. One gets the sense that this is payback time for many who have perhaps not enjoyed the most cordial of relationships with Arcadia's larger than life Chairman. There is a palpable sense that coming cap in hand for reduced rents in return for a 20% stake in the business is all a bit rich (pardon the pun!) coming from the perma-tanned tycoon. They want to be absolutely sure that there is a very realistic possibility that the business will collapse into administration if a deal is not struck. Another chapter of the so called 'retail apocalypse' being played out right in front of us. But of course, rather than being an apocalypse, this is the result of years of underinvestment in favour of extracting as much as possible from an ailing brand. Whatever the outcome, very few ever recover from a CVA, it usually spells the end. Perhaps time to make way for more relevant, interesting and exciting brands to take the place of Dorothy Perkins, Wallis and of course Topshop. As I write, this chapter is still being written.

And in the U.S. the likes of Target, Kohl's, J.Crew, Macy's and J.C. Penney are not immune from something which, at first sight, is assuming epidemic proportions. Seemingly, never a day goes by without more desperate news from the retail sector and with each wave of store closures, our thoughts inevitably turn to the loyal employees, those who have habitually got up early in the morning, or worked weekends or public holidays in order that we can shop their stores at almost any time we wish. For retail has become a 24 x 7 business and our expectations are accordingly set. But it is not only in the size and make-up of retail store estates that we are seeing some of the most emphatic changes.

I have deliberately avoided discussing much about Amazon in this book, there are plenty of column inches devoted elsewhere to that behemoth, most especially in the excellent book, *'Amazon: How the World's Most Relentless Retailer will Continue to Revolutionize Commerce'* by Natalie Berg and Miya Knights. However, it is safe to say that they will continue to disrupt the entire retail sector. Indeed, a new verb has entered our language, to be 'Amazoned', meaning the effect they have on entering any particular sector. Delivery and checkout-less stores appear to be two of the key areas set for the next round of disruption. But history tells us that trying to predict what

Amazon will do next is fraught with danger. Time will tell but disrupt they will most certainly continue to do.

And, of course there's one thing that Amazon are not saddled with, not to the extent that their high street rivals are. And that's business rates. I made several references to this throughout this book because if there's one obvious injustice pervading all of bricks and mortar retail like a disease, it is business rates. At the time of writing we are soon to get a new Prime Minister and Brexit is far from resolved therefore there seems little hope that the issue will be tackled anytime soon. But whilst it remains unresolved, the unfair pressures of unrealistic and punitive taxation levied on the high street will continue to take its prisoners. Never has there been something so unjust. It sucks the life out of retail and is a curse on all retail businesses. Creating a level playing field will, once and for all, enable all retail businesses to compete fairly, and then, only then, will we truly be able to quantify how successful or otherwise, online retailing really is.

And it is enticing to surmise how much further the growth of online will become. In 2019, in the U.K. it accounts for a little over 20% of total sales although it becomes increasingly difficult to attribute sales to either online or in-store as the customer journey becomes ever more complex. We don't think or operate in terms of channels, it is only retailers who use the term 'omnichannel' to describe theirs and our behaviour. Which is a little bizarre when one stops to think, when was the last time you ever heard someone say "I'm just off out to do a little omnichannel shopping"!

Technology

When I was running IT Services at Superdrug, many years ago I hasten to add, I was often approached by members of my team asking that we upgrade to the latest version of this desktop software or that point of sale. I used to tell them that if they wanted to play with the latest technology, they should go and work for a technology company. That was nearly twenty years ago, and oh how times change. Retail and technology are now so intertwined that sometimes it is hard to distinguish one from the other. Just look at Ocado, grocer or technology platform? And whilst retail will always, for me at least, be a human first industry, it increasingly relies on technology in order to run the business.

And it was for this reason that I deliberately included in this book some of the articles I wrote after attending retail exhibitions and conferences. For it is the smart technology decisions which will largely determine which retailers succeed and those that struggle and ultimately fall by the wayside. Customer experience and personalisation, as we know, are in danger of becoming an industry all to themselves and it is in these areas that we are beginning to see some of the most exciting advances. Retailers are now beginning to get to grips with the amount of data they are in possession of and by using technologies such as artificial intelligence and machine learning, they will be able to offer far more personal and tailored experiences for all of us.

Retail at a crossroads

Ultimately, retail is at a crossroads, a turning point brought about by the biggest disruptor of all – you and I. The very nature of what it is to be a retailer is being challenged as never before. The growth of the direct to consumer model is really asking 'why should we bother with a retailer when we can sell direct to our customers?'. All this means that the role of retail in the eco-system is under threat. But threats are renowned for also presenting opportunities.

Because there's one thing that retailers have in abundance: data. Lakes, seas, oceans of data. It's just that until very recently they haven't realised a) what to do with it and b) the strategic advantage all that data presents. We used to call it 'big data' but with the dawning of the realisation that data is the key to unlocking the secret to true personalisation, retailers are now beginning to turn big data into useful data. I was struck when talking recently to dunnhumby CEO, Guillaume Bacuvier, that they believe that with all this data at their fingertips, retailers, in many cases, will reinvent themselves more as media companies.

And with this, the very definition of 'retail' is also being challenged. Why should we define it so narrowly as to being a shopkeeper? In today's digital world, isn't retail just as much about curating experiences as well as selling products? This is where one of the great opportunities for retail lies, in expanding the definition and broadening its reach. There are many examples of where this is beginning to happen, Lululemon and Rapha immediately spring to mind. Turning their stores – in the case of Rapha – into 'clubhouses' where 'members' can socialise and simply enjoy time in each others company. If they happen to buy then so much the better but if they don't, that's OK too because maybe they will next time.

Retail apocalypse - not on my watch

Retail apocalypse? Far from it. Retail renaissance would be more fitting. And I for one can't wait to embrace it. For it promises to bring a more diverse, exciting, inspiring experience for all of us. One where 'retail' becomes an intimate part of our lives, delivering real value to us, day in day out. Yes, there will be casualties along the way but that is all part of the transformation process. When each administration is looked at a little closer, it becomes clear that they don't simply happen for no reason. And the common thread running through most is relevance. In today's ever changing, dynamic world, they were left behind, never able to recover the lost ground. I have touched on a few examples in this book.

And perhaps for all of them, they would have done no worse than to look back over a hundred years to where we came in. Because the more you study the philosophy of Harry Gordon Selfridge, the more you realise how ahead of his time he really was. What many today are touting as something new when they refer to 'experiential' retail, he was practicing to great effect all those years ago. He recognised that his eponymous store on Oxford Street was a destination long before the phrase was ever coined. He understood that his customers were more than that, just as a hotel refers to us as guests, so he treated his customers as guests when they visited his store. He understood that they were there to experience it, to meet friends, to eat, to drink, to enjoy themselves. And to this day, Selfridges is a shining example, demonstrating that if you get it right and pay attention to the things that matter, the department store model is far from dead. Because, in today's retail world, relevance and customer experience - giving us a reason to return again and again - are the keys to successful retail businesses. And in that sense, Harry truly was right all along.